Sitaare Zameen Par

-

Remedial Book for Learning Disabilities

by

Dr. Kajal Suri

Table of Contents

INTRODUCTION 11
- Seeing the Stars Among Us 11
- Why This Book Matters 12
- A Journey From Struggle to Strength 13
- A Personal Lens 14
- For Teachers, Parents, and Professionals 14
- A Vision for the Chapters Ahead 15
- Lighting Up Each Child's Sky 16

What is Specific Learning Disability? 17
- Dyslexia 21
- Dysgraphia 22
- Dyscalculia 24
- INFORMAL ASSESSMENT TOOL 27

Remediation in Writing 74
- Written Expression 75
- The Writing Connection in the Integrated Language System 75
- Early Literacy and Writing 75
- The Writing Process 76
- Stage 1: Prewriting 77
- Stage 2: Writing a Draft 77
- Stage 3: Revising 77
- Stage 4: Sharing with an Audience 78

Principles for Teaching the Writing Process (Graham et al., 2001) 78
A Learning Strategy Approach to Teaching Writing.. 79
Strategies for Writing 80
Handwriting 80
Manuscript Writing 81
Cursive Writing 81
The Left-Handed Student 81
Keyboarding 82
Graphomotor Function 82
REMEDIATION IN LANGUAGE 86
Linguistics and Language Learning 86
The Linguistic System 86
Phonology 86
Morphology 87
Syntax 87
Semantics 87
Pragmatics 88
Forms of the Language System 88
Language as a Communication Process 89
Dr. Mel Levine on Language 90
Levels of Language 90
LEVELS OF LANGUAGE PROCESSING 91
Higher Language Functioning in Early Adolescence 92
Cultural Considerations in Language Functioning in School 93

RECEPTIVE LANGUAGE 94
Five Components of Receptive Language 95
Common Indicators of Possible Receptive Language Weaknesses 99
Expressive Language 100
Six Components of Expressive Language............ 101
Common Indicators of Possible Expressive Language Weaknesses 104
Spelling.. 106
Difficulties with Spelling.................................... 106
Word Sorts... 107
Word Builder 108
Word Wall.. 108
Process for Learning New Words 109
Tricky Words 110
Mnemonics 112
MNEMONICS – BRAINTRICKS 114
Finally... 115
Reading Strategies 116
Why is reading important?.................................. 116
Reading Problems Noted Among Students with LD 116
Conceptualization of Reading Skills 117
WORD ATTACK SKILLS 117
PHONICS.. 118

A REVIEW OF COMMON PHONIC GENERALIZATIONS 119
Consonants 119
Consonants c and g 119
Consonant Blends 120
Consonant Digraphs 120
Silent Consonants 121
Vowels 121
Short vowel sounds 122
Long vowels 122
Double Vowels: Vowel Digraph 122
Final e / Magic e 123
Vowels Modified by r 123
Diphthongs 124
Syllabication 125
Number of Syllables 125
Sight Words 125
Word Comprehension 126
Strategies for Improving Reading Fluency 126
Sentence Comprehension 127
Comprehension of Longer Texts 127
Activating Background Knowledge 128
Building Vocabulary and Concepts 129
Expanding Vocabulary 130
Providing Concrete Experiences 130
Cloze Procedure 131

Sub-skills to Be Emphasized in Comprehension .. 131
DYSCALCULIA REMEDIAL STRATEGIES.................. 135
LANGUAGE 135
PERCEPTION.. 136
ATTENTION 138
NUMBER PROCESSING 138
Counting... 140
Number Concepts 141
Place Value Strategies 141
Addition Strategies 142
Subtraction Strategies 143
MULTIPLICATION 143
Division... 144
Fractions 145
Time 146
Decimals 147
Integers and Algebra 148
Procedural Skills 149
Mathematical Reasoning 150
General Tips.. 151
INDIVIDUALISED EDUCATION PROGRAM (IEP) 153
EIGHT Basic Components of an Individualized Education Program 154
Developing an IEP... 163
IEP Planning Form – Sample 166
CONCLUSION 168

Lighting Pathways for Every Learner 168
From Understanding to Action 169
The Role of Empathy and Observation 170
Collaboration: The Strength of the System 171
Celebrating Progress, Not Perfection 171
A New Way of Seeing Children 172
A Final Reflection 173

INTRODUCTION

Seeing the Stars Among Us

Every child who walks into a classroom carries an entire universe within-an evolving constellation of thoughts, memories, strengths, curiosities, and struggles. Yet, in the fast-moving rhythm of schools and the pressure to meet academic standards, many bright young minds slip through unnoticed, not because they lack potential, but because their stars shine differently. *Sitaare Zameen Par* was born from the need to look upward-and inward-to rediscover these stars, understand their patterns, and help them glow in their own distinct brilliance.

Across classrooms, we see children who speak fluently yet freeze when asked to write; children who can solve practical problems but stumble over written word problems; children who express ideas with creativity but cannot recall the sequence of steps in a math exercise; and others who listen attentively but struggle to decode text. None of these difficulties diminish their intelligence. Instead, they reveal how diverse and complex human learning truly is. Recognizing this diversity is the foundation of meaningful education.

For years, teachers, therapists, and parents have searched for ways to bridge the gap between what a child *knows* and what a child can *express*. This book aims to become that bridge. It draws from research-based practices, everyday classroom realities, and deep psychosocial understanding to illuminate the world of literacy, language, numeracy, cognition, and learning differences. More importantly, it translates theory into practical steps-tools that busy teachers, overwhelmed parents, and dedicated educators can use immediately.

Just as a star's glow is shaped by physics, environment, distance, and energy, a child's learning is shaped by multiple systems-language, memory, motor skills, attention, emotional development, sociocultural context, and the environment in which learning takes place. A child who struggles to copy from the board may not be careless; they may be battling weak graphomotor memory. A child who misinterprets instructions may not be inattentive; they could be wrestling with receptive language processing. And a child who stares blankly at numbers may not dislike math; they may simply need a different way of experiencing quantity, sequence, or spatial meaning.

Understanding these nuances is not only educational-it is transformative.

Why This Book Matters

In many educational settings, skills like reading, writing, spelling, and mathematics are taught as if they exist in isolation. But children do not learn that way. Learning is a deeply interwoven process. When a student writes, they draw upon oral language, memory, motor control, visual perception, sequencing, and vocabulary. When a student reads, they rely on rhythmic coordination between phonological awareness, semantic understanding, and syntactic processing. When they attempt a math problem, they depend on language comprehension, attention, and spatial organization.

This book recognizes these interdependencies and offers a holistic understanding of how learning unfolds in real life. It takes readers behind the scenes of what appears to be "simple tasks" and uncovers the layered skills that underpin them. The goal is not just to identify what a child cannot do, but to understand *why*-and then chart a pathway forward.

A Journey From Struggle to Strength

Through the chapters that follow, you will step into the world of early literacy, the science of writing, the mechanics of reading, the intricacies of graphomotor development, and the cognitive demands of mathematics. You will explore how children understand language, why they confuse sounds, how they decode symbols, why handwriting becomes laborious, and how their emotional responses shape academic behavior.

You will also meet children through illustrative scenarios-students who remind us of those we've taught, lived with, or loved. You may recognize the hesitant writer who maps ideas in their mind but struggles to put pencil to paper; the thoughtful reader who understands stories when read aloud but falters when decoding independently; the bright child who grasps mathematical concepts in conversation yet freezes during timed tests.

Every scenario serves a dual purpose: to deepen empathy and sharpen instructional strategy.

A Personal Lens

Many years ago, I observed a child who would drift quietly to the back of the classroom during writing sessions. He rarely volunteered, often appeared lost, and avoided eye contact when worksheets were handed out. One afternoon, during a conversation at recess, he animatedly explained the rules of a game he had invented-complete with characters, strategies, and imaginary landscapes. His verbal richness contrasted sharply with his written work.

That moment changed the way I looked at "performance." His struggle was not a lack of intelligence but a mismatch between the way he processed language and the way he was expected to show his learning. Once we replaced lengthy writing tasks with verbal mapping, kinesthetic prompts, and scaffolded graphic organizers, the same child began producing work he felt proud of.

Experiences like this-small yet profound-remind us that children do not fail learning; sometimes learning fails to meet children where they are.

For Teachers, Parents, and Professionals

This book speaks to anyone committed to helping children learn:

- Teachers who want practical tools that genuinely work in diverse classrooms

- Parents seeking clarity and reassurance as they support their children at home
- Special educators designing interventions, accommodations, and IEP goals
- Counselors and therapists collaborating to build holistic support systems
- School leaders striving to create inclusive, empathetic learning environments

Each chapter builds upon the last, creating a tapestry of actionable understanding-whether you are grappling with phonics or morphology, supporting handwriting or comprehension, teaching number sense or addressing dyscalculia, or developing a child's social-language competencies.

A Vision for the Chapters Ahead

Through the pages of *Sitaare Zameen Par*, you will:

- Learn how language functions across multiple levels and why mastery requires more than vocabulary.
- Understand the writing process as a developmental journey rather than a simple skill.
- Explore the interconnection between reading fluency, phonological awareness, and comprehension.

- Discover the complexities of mathematical reasoning and how children construct number meaning.
- Gain tools for identifying early signs of learning differences and creating targeted support.
- Learn to design meaningful, achievable, and child-centered IEPs.

This book is designed to be both a guide and a companion-something you can return to whenever a child's learning puzzle seems difficult to solve.

Lighting Up Each Child's Sky

In the end, *Sitaare Zameen Par* is a reminder that children do not need to change their nature to fit into fixed educational molds. Instead, educators and environments must evolve to recognize the brightness each child brings. When we pause long enough to understand how a child thinks, how they process information, and what their learning pathways look like, we do more than teach-we illuminate.

Every page invites you to look up, observe closely, and notice the stars that have always been there. Our task is simple yet profound: help them shine-boldly, proudly, and in their own unique constellation.

What is Specific Learning Disability?

A Specific Learning Disability (SLD) is a neurological (brain-based) condition that affects how a person processes, stores, or uses information, making it hard to learn and use certain academic skills—even though the child's intelligence is average or above average, and they have had appropriate teaching opportunities.

In simple words:

- **The child is capable and intelligent**
- **But learns in a different way**
- And needs **special strategies and support** to succeed

Key Features of Specific Learning Disability

A child may have SLD when they show persistent difficulty in one or more of these areas:

1) Reading (Dyslexia)

- Trouble recognizing words
- Slow reading speed
- Weak comprehension due to decoding difficulty
- Confusing similar letters/words (b/d, was/saw)

2) Writing (Dysgraphia)

- Poor handwriting

- Difficulty forming letters
- Weak spelling
- Trouble organizing ideas into written sentences

3) Mathematics (Dyscalculia)

- Difficulty understanding numbers and quantity
- Confusion with steps in calculations
- Problems with place value, time, money, fractions

What SLD is NOT

SLD is **not caused by**:

- laziness
- poor parenting
- low intelligence
- lack of motivation
- hearing/vision problems (though these should be ruled out)

Also, SLD is **different from**:

- Intellectual Disability (low IQ)
- ADHD (attention difficulty—may co-exist)

- Autism (social + communication patterns—may co-exist)
- Emotional disturbance (though frustration can develop)

Why it Happens

SLD happens because the brain processes certain information differently, especially:

- language sounds (phonological processing)
- memory and sequencing
- visual-motor coordination
- processing speed
- working memory

This is why a child might understand something orally but struggle when reading or writing it.

Common Signs of SLD

A child may:

- read slowly or avoid reading
- spell poorly even after practice
- write very slowly or with messy handwriting
- forget steps in math

- struggle with copying from the board
- take longer than peers to complete work
- have strong oral skills but weak written output

Diagnosis and Support

SLD is usually identified through:

- academic performance patterns
- teacher observations
- standardized testing and psycho-educational assessments

Support includes:

- special teaching methods (phonics, structured writing)
- accommodations (extra time, reader, scribe, calculator)
- individualized education plan (IEP)
- therapy (occupational therapy for handwriting, etc.)

Most Important Point

A child with SLD can absolutely succeed when taught using the right approach. Many children with SLD are highly creative, logical, artistic, or verbally strong—they simply need a learning pathway that matches their brain.

Dyslexia

Specific Learning Disability (SLD) is a neurological condition in which the brain's language-processing areas function differently because of variations in brain wiring. It often runs in families. Children with dyslexia are usually bright and capable, but they experience difficulties in academic skills—especially those that depend on language. Specific Learning Disabled children typically have average or above-average IQ and adequate mental ability, but they show a significant gap between their potential and actual academic performance. Learning disability may also be understood as a kind of helplessness a student experiences when they repeatedly struggle with school tasks despite effort.

According to the National Advisory Committee on Handicapped Children (USA), a specific learning disability refers to a disorder in one or more of the basic psychological processes involved in understanding or using language, spoken or written. This may show itself as an imperfect ability to listen, think, speak, read, write, spell, or perform mathematical calculations.

Dyslexia is one of the most commonly found learning disabilities. It mainly affects reading, writing, and spelling, because the child faces difficulty in the language-processing system of the brain. Children with dyslexia may show weakness in reading, such as difficulty decoding words, understanding sound-letter associations, and reading fluently, even though their intelligence is normal. The challenges seen in dyslexia can vary widely from one child to another and are often linked to differences in language processing related to visual memory, auditory memory, visual perception, and auditory perception.

Many children with dyslexia also struggle with spelling, because the input information they process is often unclear or inaccurate, which leads to incorrect written output. Some children have difficulty understanding and recalling information in the correct sequence, which affects their performance in comprehension, grammar, and written expression. Common symptoms include skipping words while reading, spelling the same word in different ways, mixing up letters or sounds, and writing incorrect spellings due to confusion between phonetic patterns and letter forms.

Dysgraphia

Dysgraphia is a neurological learning disorder that mainly affects a child's ability to write clearly and efficiently. It causes difficulty with handwriting, letter formation, spelling, and sometimes even with putting thoughts into written words—despite the child having normal or above-average intelligence. One of the most noticeable signs is poor handwriting, but dysgraphia is not simply "messy writing." It is a deeper difficulty in the brain's ability to coordinate the skills needed for writing.

Children with dysgraphia often struggle with the physical mechanics of writing. They may hold the pencil awkwardly, use too much or too little pressure, have an unstable grip between the thumb and fingers, or position the paper incorrectly—sometimes tilting or slanting it in unusual ways. Because of these visible difficulties, many children are misunderstood as being careless, lazy, or not trying hard enough, when in reality the writing process is genuinely demanding for them. Dysgraphia commonly occurs along with other conditions such as ADHD and autism, which can further affect attention, motor control, and written expression.

In the elementary school years, writing clearly and correctly becomes an important part of academic achievement. When handwriting is slow, uncomfortable, or confusing, it can affect a child's performance across subjects, because writing is required not only in language tasks but also in mathematics, science, and classroom assessments. Dysgraphia can interfere significantly with learning during the early academic years, especially when the child is expected to write longer sentences, copy from the board, or complete written exams within a time limit.

There are **different types of dysgraphia**, and a child may show features of more than one type:

- **Dyslexic dysgraphia** is related to difficulties in the language areas of the brain. The child struggles to connect how words **sound** with how they should **look in written form**. This affects spelling and written expression, even if handwriting is sometimes legible.

- **Motor dysgraphia** is linked to weak **fine motor skills** and poor muscle control needed for handwriting. The child finds it difficult to hold a pencil properly, form letters smoothly, and write without fatigue.

- **Spatial dysgraphia** is connected to difficulty understanding the **space and layout** required for writing. Children may leave unusually large gaps between letters and words, struggle to write on a line, and often face difficulty with drawing because they cannot judge spacing on paper accurately.

- **Phonological dysgraphia** involves trouble connecting how words **sound** to how they are **spelled**. The child may miswrite words because the brain struggles to process and organize language sounds correctly.

With appropriate support—such as occupational therapy, handwriting interventions, keyboarding options, extra time, and structured writing strategies—children with dysgraphia can improve their writing skills and feel more confident in expressing what they know.

Dyscalculia

Dyscalculia is a neurological learning disability that affects a child's ability to understand and work with numbers and mathematical concepts. It is often described as a "math learning disorder," and in everyday language some people call it "math dyslexia," although it is a distinct condition. Dyscalculia can appear in children with normal or above-average intelligence, but they struggle significantly with number sense, calculation, and mathematical reasoning. It may also co-occur with conditions like ADHD and autism, which can influence attention, memory, and learning performance.

Research has shown that dyscalculia is related to differences in the brain regions responsible for learning, memory, decision-making, and number processing. Using brain imaging tools, researchers have identified changes in grey matter, and variations in brain surface area, thickness, and volume in areas connected to mathematical thinking. Genetics also plays a role—if a parent has had difficulties with mathematics or learning-related challenges, the child may have a higher risk of developing dyscalculia.

One of the most common difficulties in dyscalculia is trouble with counting and number tracking. Children may lose their place while counting, count the same objects repeatedly, or struggle to understand number sequences. Many children with dyscalculia continue to rely on finger counting long after peers of the same age have moved on to mental calculation strategies. They may also struggle with a skill called subitizing, which is the ability to quickly recognize how many objects are in a small group without counting one-by-one. Subitizing is an essential foundation skill for mathematical operations such as addition and subtraction, and weakness in this area makes calculations harder and slower.

Dyscalculia can also affect basic number understanding in ways that seem surprising. Some children find it difficult to grasp simple comparisons, such as knowing instantly that 5 is greater than 3, or recognizing which of two numbers is larger. For many children, numbers can trigger strong anxiety, especially when math activities are repeated without the correct support. This anxiety may cause avoidance behaviors, emotional frustration, or low confidence, and can affect not only school performance but also daily life tasks.

Children with dyscalculia may struggle in everyday situations that involve numbers, time, and direction. They may confuse right and left, mix up sequences or numeric details such as addresses, forget directions, and have trouble judging distance or estimating time. For example, they may not realize how long they have spent in the shower or how much time is needed to get ready. Dyscalculia can also cause difficulties with remembering and using numbers such as phone numbers, house addresses, or even numeric information related to close relatives.

With proper intervention—such as structured step-by-step teaching, visual models, number line work, repeated practice in small manageable steps, and supportive accommodations—children with dyscalculia can improve their skills and become more confident in mathematics. The key is early identification, consistent support, and teaching methods that match the child's learning style rather than forcing one standard approach.

INFORMAL ASSESSMENT TOOL

Index

⇒Introduction

⇒Visual perception

1. Figure ground perception
2. Form constancy perception
3. Visual discrimination
4. Visual closure
5. Position in space perception
6. Visual spatial perception
7. Visual sequential memory
8. Visual non sequential memory

⇒Auditory perception

1. Auditory figure ground
2. auditory discrimination
3. auditory blending
4. auditory analysis
5. auditory closure
6. auditory sequential memory
7. auditory and non sequential memory

⇒Language

1. Receptive language
2. listening comprehension
3. reading comprehension
4. expressive language
5. oral expression
6. written expression

⇒Mathematics

⇒Graphomotor skills

⇒Logical and abstract reasoning skills

⇒Rubrics and final scoring

Introduction to informal assessment

An informal assessment is spontaneous. it is a method of evaluation where the instructor test participant's knowledge using no standard criteria or or specifically designed rubrics. structure simply ask open ended questions and observe student performance to determine how much they know. Sawmill assessments are done with help of standardized test whereas informal assessments are content and performances driven which are tailor made by special educators.

This approach encourages the students to produce construct demonstrate or perform a response. these measures are useful and practical assessment procedures that test student on the ordinary material and activities that they are currently working with classroom. this test also gave the teacher freedom in administration and interpretation example extra time adjustment put student at is and help ensure that they will give their best efforts. formal assessment can also be conducted more frequently than the formal assessment.

Informal assessment are observational tools which can assess teacher in identifying students strength and weaknesses and in Planning future lessons. It is very beneficial resource that gave book teacher and student a quick glance for making required changes for immediate decisions. these methods may be helpful if teacher want to decide which student will work independently for which students requires constant support. Another important aspect of informal assessment is that they actively involve the students in the evaluation process which help teacher to understand the students present level and plan the lessons accordingly.

Visual discrimination

Level 1

Circle the picture that does not belong in each group. Following are the 5 groups/questions given to choose from and it is 2 marks each.

Visual discrimination

Level 2

Make the child learn 5 shapes, circle, square, triangle, pentagon, hexagon. Now the child has to connect the shapes merged together in the first picture to the shapes given in front of them. (2 marks for every right shape)

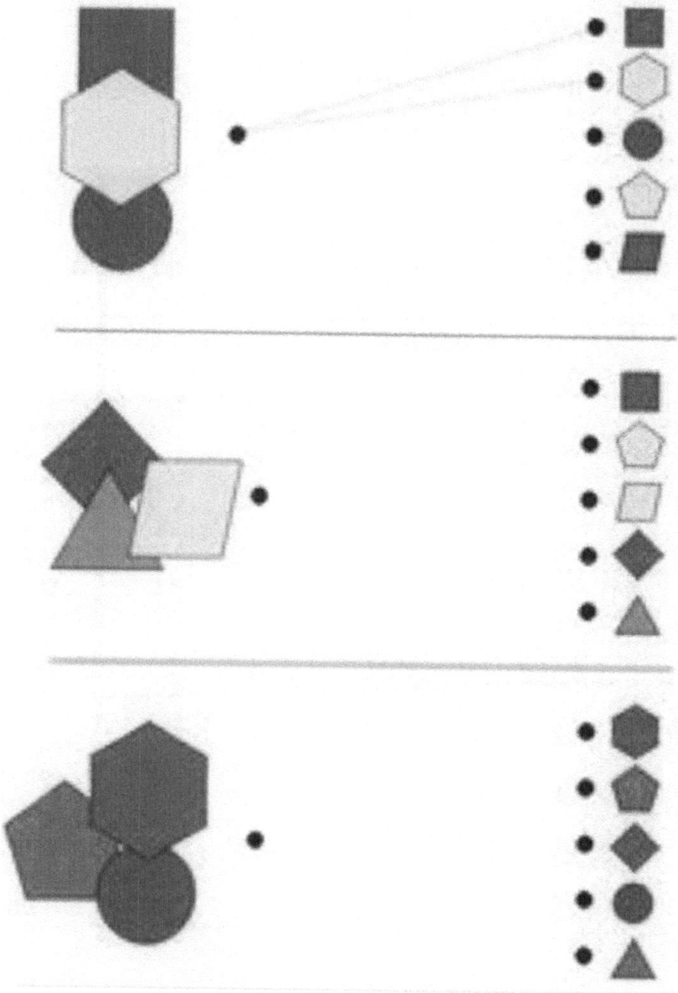

Visual figure ground perception

Level 1

Visual figure ground perception

Level 2

Visual Spatial skills

Level 1

There are 5 questions given below. The child has to mark the cat that matches the word. (2 marks for each right answer)

left

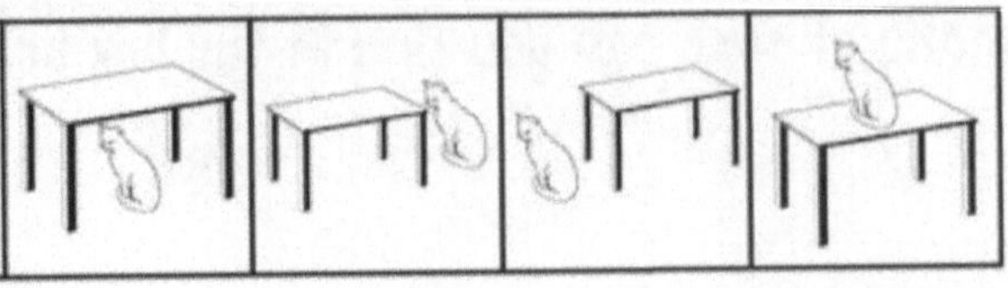

right

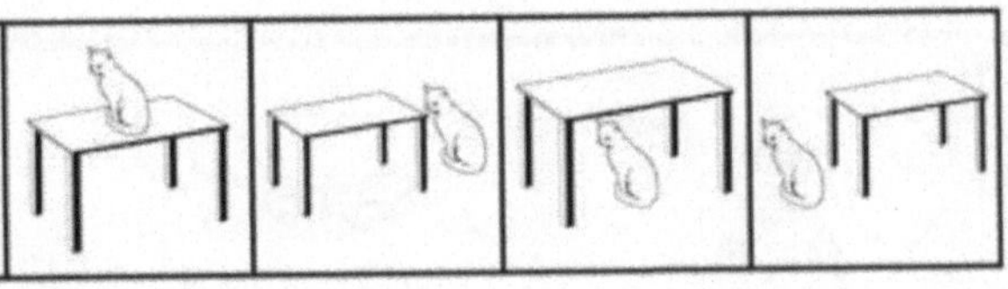

on top

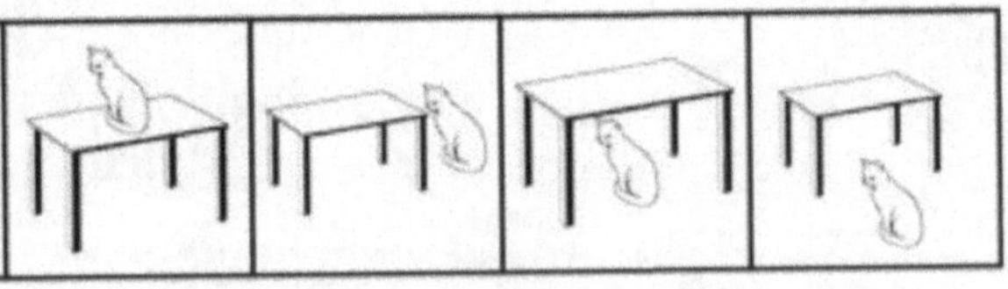

under

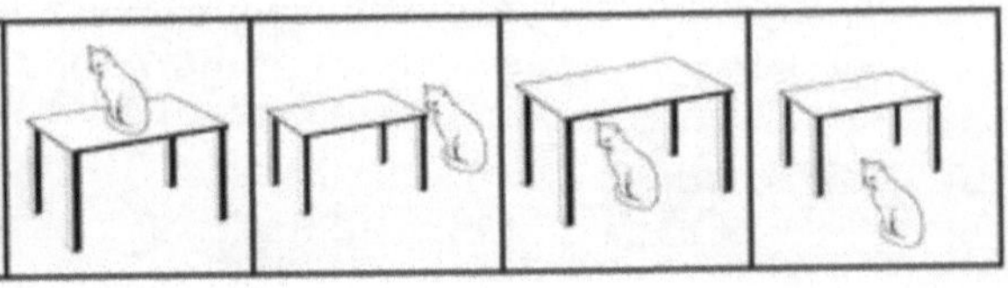

in front

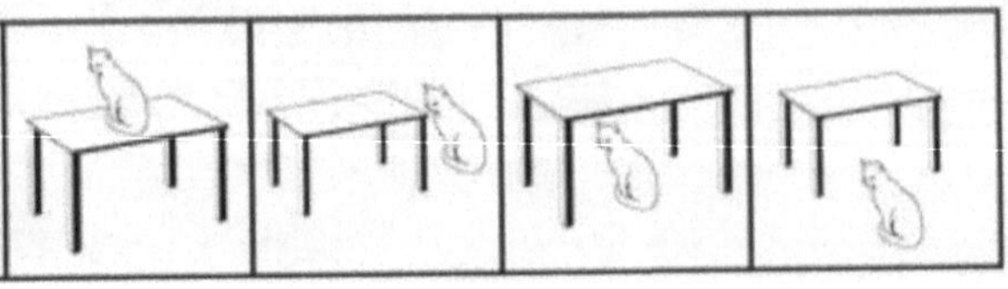

Visual spatial skills

Level 2

There are 5 questions given below. The child has to mark the circle that matches the word. (2 marks each for every right answer)

under	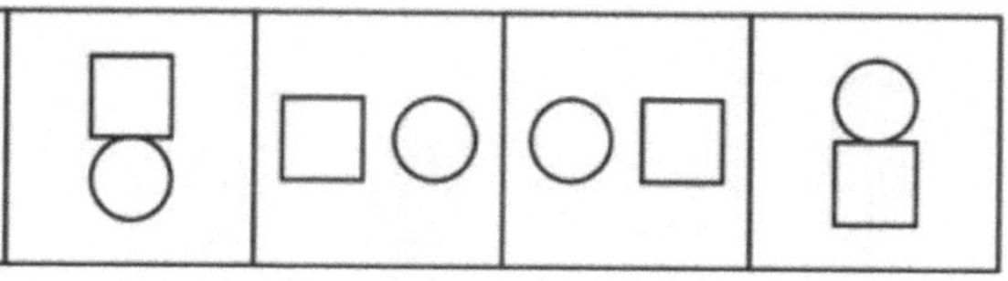
on top	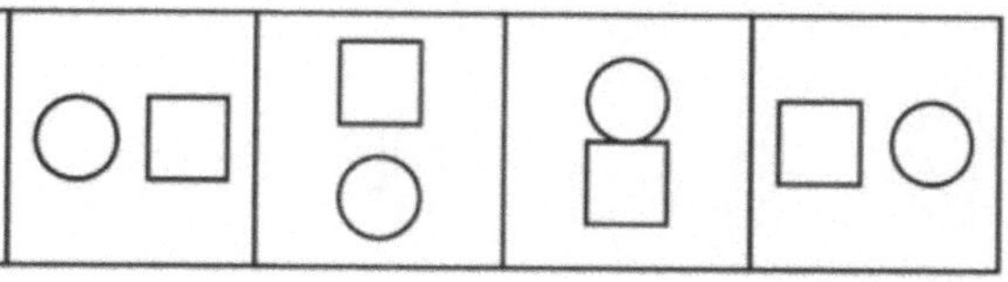
left	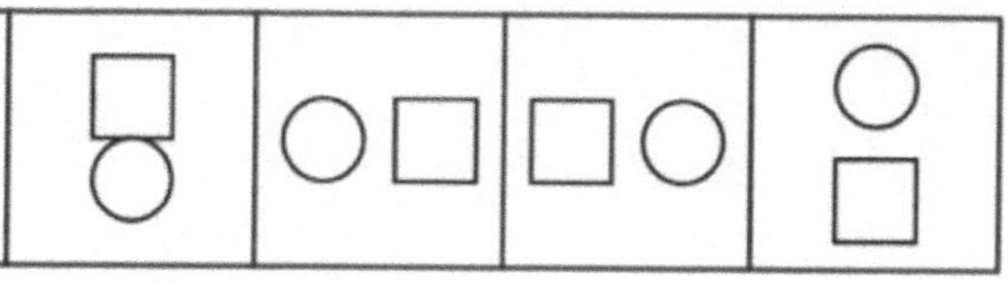
above	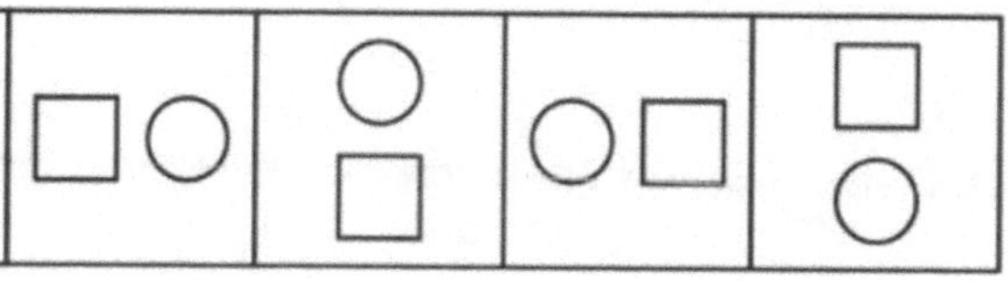
below	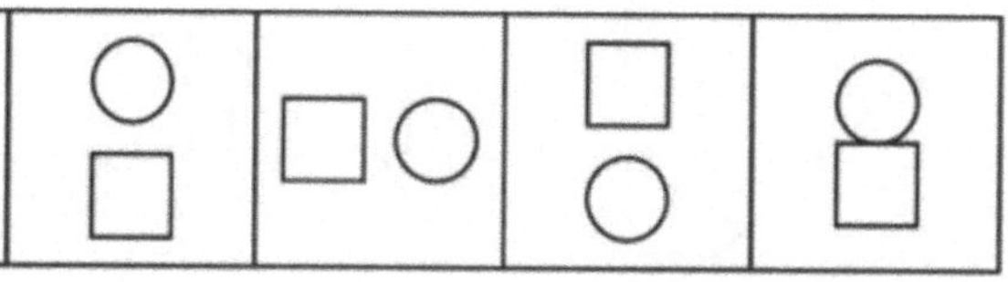

Visual form constancy

Level 1

There are four different color arrows given below similarly the child has to color all the arrows given below in the specific color related to their direction.

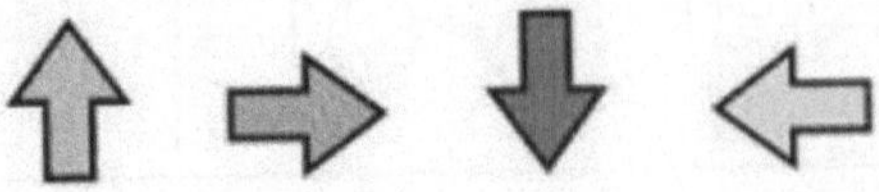

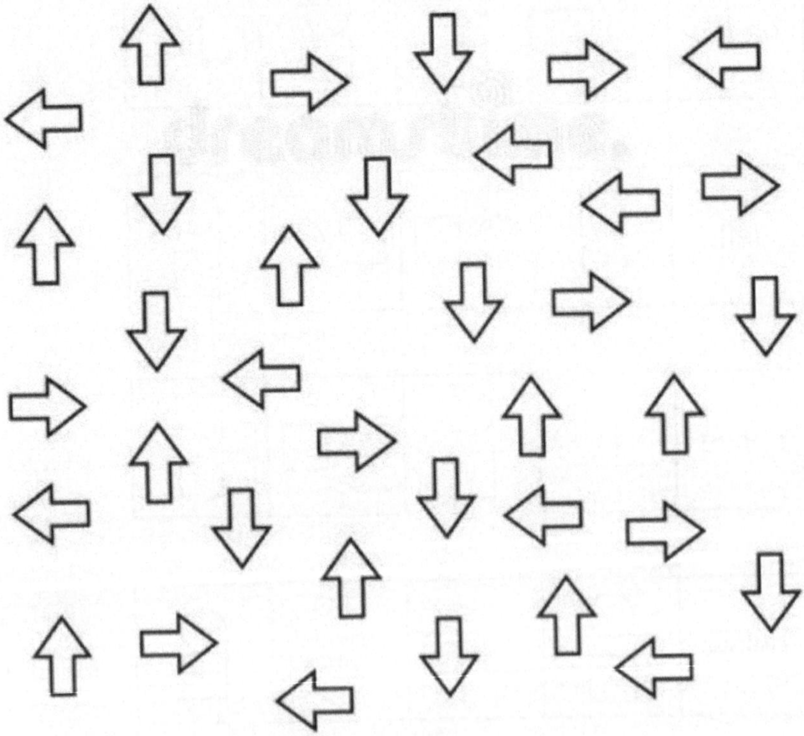

Visual form constancy

Level 2

In each row circle the letter that is the same as the first letter.

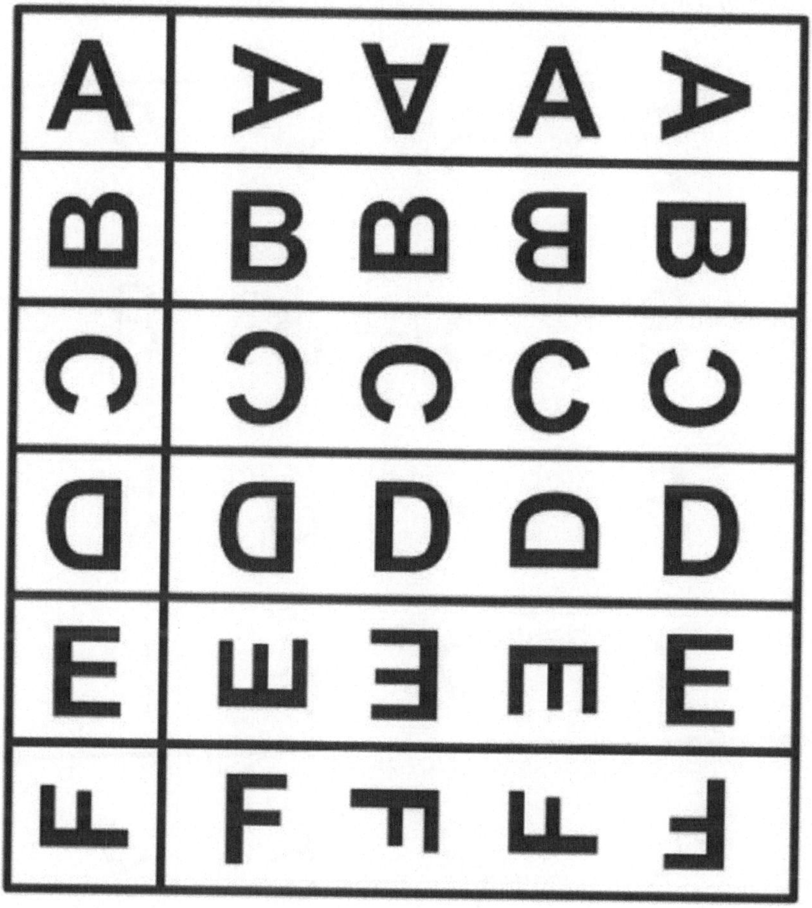

Visual closure

Level 1

There are 5 questions given below. Which number would be the same as the example if you completed the missing part? (2 marks for each right answer)

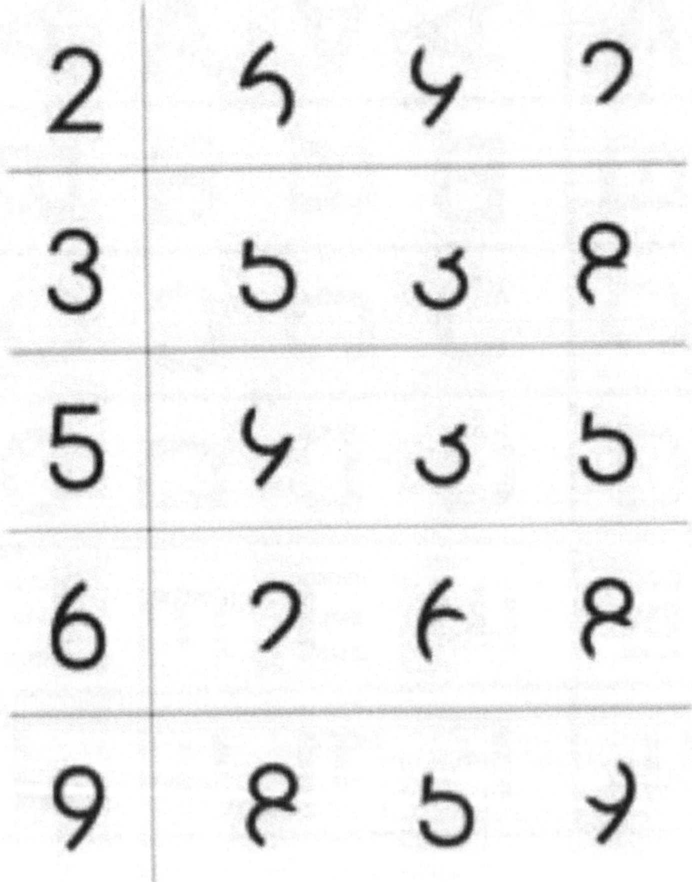

Visual closure

Level 2

There are 8 shapes given below. The child has to give the closure by completing all the following shapes.

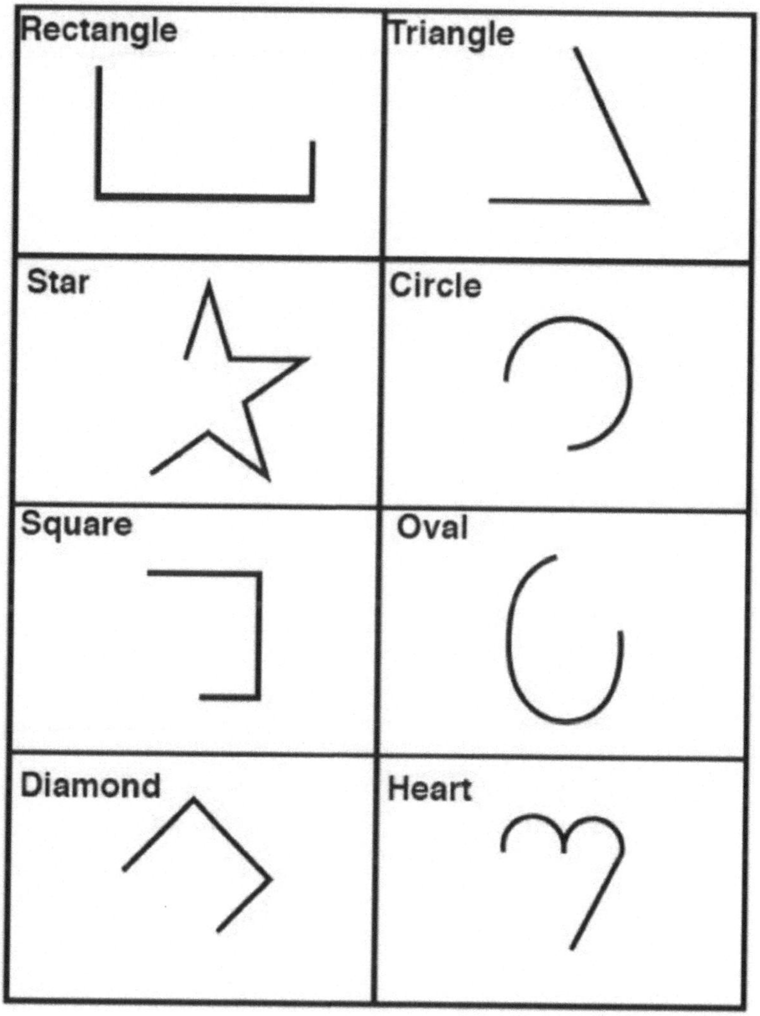

Visual sequential memory

Level 1

Child has to try to remember the order of each of the following design and then teacher will cover the designs are and tell the child to copy them to the empty blocks.

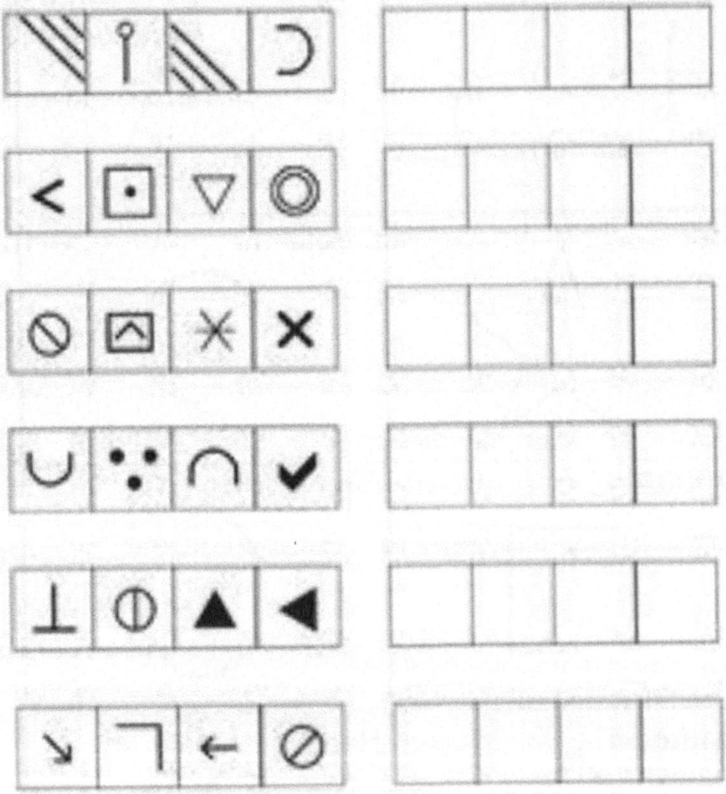

Visual sequential memory

level 2

There is a row of pictures after i cover the pictures i want u to tell me exactly each time the pictures you saw. Try to tell in the same order.

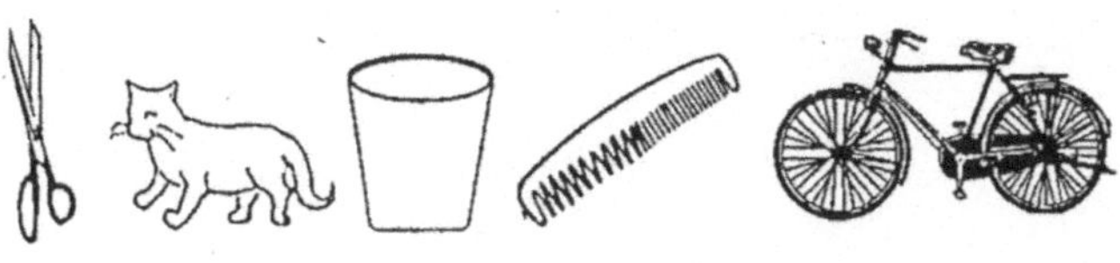

Auditory figure ground perception

level-1

Tell the following words to the child and child is expected to say if their same or different if child make some mistake a second presentation could be made of the same words if he fails again it can be counted as an error 54 more uncorrected errors by childs age 6 or older suggest difficulty with auditory discrimination.

1. shine - sign
2. tin - thin
3. mob - mop
4. ship - sip
5. goal - coal
6. bus - buzz
7. mud - mug
8. bill - mill
9. deck - dock
10. mash - mush

Auditory figure ground perception

Level 2

Tell the following words to the child and child is expected to say if their same or different if child make some mistake a second presentation could be made of the same words if he fails again it can be counted as an error 54 more uncorrected errors by childs age 6 or older suggest difficulty with auditory discrimination.

1. ate - eight
2. bare - bear
3. blew - blue
4. cereal - serial
5. flour - flower
6. hole - whole
7. knot - not
8. wear - where
9. tail - tale
10. threw - through

Auditory discrimination

Sound identification activity

level 1

DB sound identification activity e where in teacher will play a sound game with children. Fix a board order divided behind which a sound can be created. itAsk the children to identify the all different sounds by just hearing it .

Suggestions

Clap your hands

Tear a piece of paper

Cut paper with scissors

Bounce a ball

snap your finger

click a camera

Pop a balloon

staple a paper

Auditory discrimination

Sound identification activity

level 2

Teacher will play a game with the children.Use Old film container for small plastic bottles that had been washed out. Fill two of each container with the same level of rice beans stones etc. Hot- glue the lids to secured them. child to tell you why he thinks they match child has to discriminate between the two sounds. Now listen to the child reasoning carefully.

If you use a clear bottle cover it with paper. big box stores still get film containers.

Auditory blending
Level 1

Auditory blending is the ability to synthesize the individual sounds phonemes of a word so that the whole world can be recognised.
Look at the picture given below and colour the right blend then write the right blanks sound to complete the word.

dr / br  d r e s s	fr / tr  _ _ e e
gr / br  _ _ e a d	br / gr  _ _ a s s
cr / gr  _ _ a y o n	tr / dr  _ _ a s h
br / fr  _ _ o g	cr / gr  _ _ a b
gr / cr  _ _ a p e s	pr / br 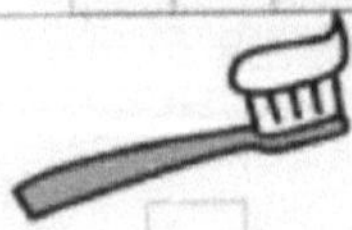 _ _ u s h

Auditory blending
level 2

Writer correct S blend from the given box and complete the word following.

st	sp	sh	sn	st	sw	sp	sl

 ....ake	 ....oon
 ....oes	 ....own
 ....rawberry	 ....ar
 ....an	 ....irt
 ....ain	 ....ider
 ....ip	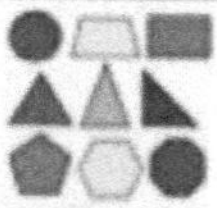 ....ape
 ....ide	 ....op

Auditory closure
level 1

Auditory closure is the ability to use redundant intrinsic and extrinsic qualities of speech in order to fill in missing segment so that the complete message can be understood. following are the short sentences given tell the child to read them out and complete them.

On thanksgiving, we eat _____.

A. Turkey
B. Hamburgers
C. Pasta

I want to play a _____.

A. B all
B. Game
C. Frog

I like need to cut the paper with ____.

A. Knife
B. Bottle
C. Scissors

After dinner, my mom and dad wash the _____.

A. Dishes
B. Laundry
C. Toys

____ live in the ocean.

A. Cows
B. Fish
C. Elephants

On ____ I dress up in a costume.

A. Easter
B. 4th of July
C. Halloween

Auditory closure
level 2

Auditory closure is the ability to use redundant intrinsic and extrinsic qualities of speech in order to fill in missing segment so that the complete message can be understood. following are the short sentences given tell the child to read them out and complete them.

I forgot to bring my math book home from school so I can't to my _____

A. Homework
B. Craft project
C. Video game

communicationstationspeechtx.blogspot.com

My sister woke up with a high fever today. My mom made her a _____ appointment.

A. Veterinary
B. Doctor's
C. Library

communicationstationspeechtx.blogspot.com

My brother didn't eat his dinner last night, so he woke up this morning feeling very ___.

A. Hungry
B. Tired
C. Hurt

communicationstationspeechtx.blogspot.com

I fell and scraped my knee. My mom cleaned my boo, boo and put a ___ on it.

A. Scratch
B. Band aid
C. Sticker

communicationstationspeechtx.blogspot.com

Auditory sequential memory
level 1

Directions

"I am going to read some sentences to you. When I finish, just repeat w h a t I said".

1. The boy has a ball. -
2. I like to sit in t h e car.
3. Last Sunday we went for a movie
4. Ramu is going to the market.
5. I like to go to school.

80

6. Sita is dancing.
7. I like to eat sweets.
8. It is raining heavily

One or more errors in each of the eight sentences suggests difficulty with auditory memory in children age 5.

A child of 6 years can repeat atleast five sentences without any error.

Supplement your test findings with behavioural observations/information obtained from parents.

— may have difficulty in following a sequence of directions at home or in school.

able to understand and to recognise words but has difficulty retrieving them.

parents complain that what they told him yesterday, has been forgotten today.

Auditory sequential memory
level 2

Directions

"I am going to read some sentences to you. When I finish, just repeat w h a t I said".

1. The boy went to play football.
2. I like to sit in the car and peek out of the window
3. Last Sunday we went to the market and shopped for groceries
4. Ramu is going to the market as instructed by Vinita
5. I like to go to school and study with my peers
6. Sita is dancing swiftly with her friends
7. I like to eat something sweet after my meals
8. The forecast shows that it is going to rain heavily.

One or more errors in each of the eight sentences suggests difficulty with auditory memory in children age 5.

A child of 6 years can repeat atleast five sentences without any error.

Supplement your test findings with behavioural observations/information obtained from parents.

— may have difficulty in following a sequence of directions at home or in school.

able to understand and to recognise words but has difficulty retrieving them.

parents complain that what they told him yesterday, has been forgotten today.

Language assessment

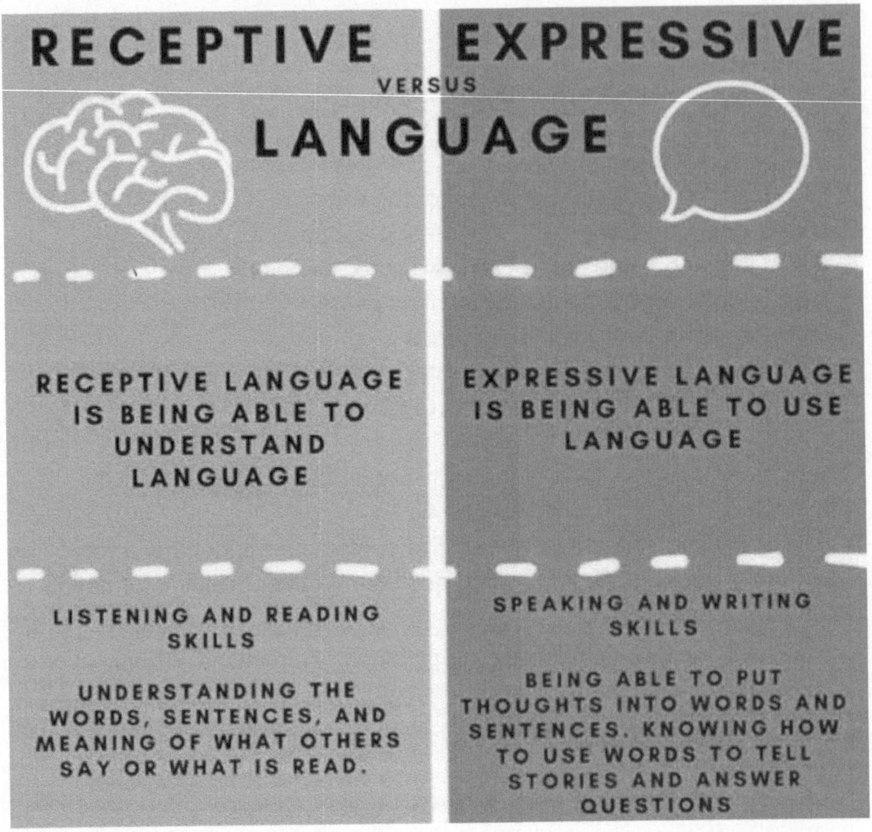

Receptive language listening comprehension level 1

Name: ______________________ **Date:** ___________

Story Elements - Character, Setting, Plot

Directions: Listen as your teacher read the story. Choose the correct answer for each question.

A Trip to the Nurse

Tony's class was playing kickball for recess. He was having so much fun! When the ball went flying into the air, he quickly ran to catch it. Instead of catching the ball, the ball hit Tony's head. Tony fell to the ground. "My head really hurts," he told his teacher. Tony's teacher walked him to the school nurse. She gave Tony an ice pack for his head. Soon, his head began to feel better.

1. Who were the characters in the story?
(a) Tammy (b) Tony (c) Teacher (d) nurse

2. Who was the main character in the story?
(a) Tammy (b) Tony (c) Teacher

3. What is the setting of the story?
(a) Football field (b) Home (c) Park (d) school

4. How does the character feel at the end of the story?
(a) Happy (b) Sleepy (c) Sad

5. What is the problem in the story?
(a) The ball hit Tony hit.
(b) They were playing at recess time.
(c) They walked to the nurse office.

6. How was the problem solved?
(a) Tony went to class (b) Tony went to the nurse

Receptive language listening comprehension level 2

Monday is my favourite day! This is what I usually do on Mondays.

I get up at quarter to 1.............., I eat my breakfast and at half past eight I go to 2................. I sometimes ride my bike to school.

I like Mondays, because at nine o'clock we have English! At half past twelve it's 3...................... I always eat lunch at school. At quarter to two I have Music. I like Music! It's interesting! I go home at half past three

In the afternoon, I always do my 4......................... Then, at quarter to seven, I watch 'Queen Street' on TV, but I never go to bed 5................ I always go to bed at half past nine!

What's the time?

It's

It's

It's

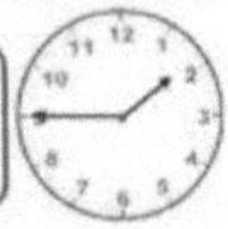

It's

It's

Answer the questions.

1. What's the girl's favourite day?
2. What time does she get up?
3. How does she get to school?
4. Does she like Music?
5. When does she do her homework?
6. What TV show does she watch?

True or false

1. She gets up at quarter to eight.
2. She goes to school by bus.
3. She has Art at nine o'clock.
4. She does her homework in the afternoon.
5. She watches TV in the evening.
6. She always goes to bed late.

Ask and answer.

1 What's your favourite day?
2 What's your favourite subject?
3 What do you usually eat for breakfast?
4 What time do you go to school?
5 What do you usually do in the evening?
6 What time do you go to bed?
7 What do you usually do on Sundays?

Ask and answer.

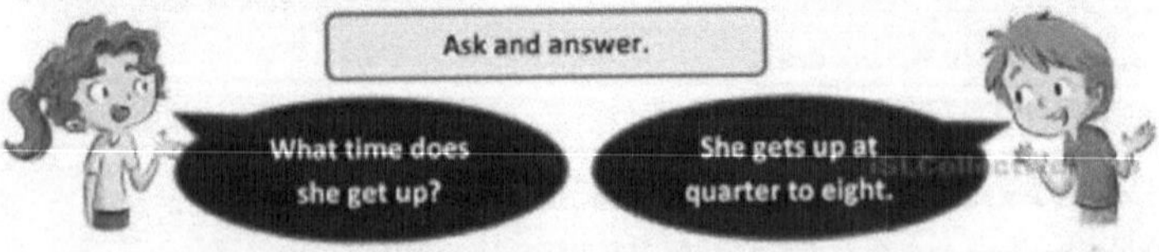

Receptive language reading comprehension level 1

What If....?

Read the story below.

Nandi sat on the blue steps of her house. She was wondering..... What if jelly beans made you jump really high? You could get to school in one big leap! What if houses were rocket ships? Your family could go holidays to the moon! What if the pictures in books flew around your head when Dad read to you? What if my pink gumboots were magical? I could run faster than my big brother! "Nandi, what are you doing?"Asked Nandi's big brother. Nandi sat back on the step with a big smile on her face. "Just wondering," she said.

Answer each question.

1. What Nandi was wondering about the jelly beans?

 ____

2. What do you wonder when Dad read to you?

 ____

3. Why did Nandi think that her pink gumboots were magical?

 ____

4. "Nandi what are you doing?" Who said that?

 a. Mum   b. Big brother   c. Dad

5. What if the flowers could talk? What would they say?

 ____

Receptive language
reading comprehension
level 2

Q. Reading Comprehension

Anna's lute

Anna's favorite hobby is playing lute. She spends a lot of her free time playing lute. She started learning to play lute when she was 5 years old. She played in her school's band.

Anna's dad bought her a lute and she started practicing every day after school. It was very loud, but her mother never complained. She improved a lot, and playing lute has been her favorite hobby ever since.

1) What is Anna's favorite hobby?

____

2) When did Anna start to play lute?

____

3) Who bought Anna a lute?

____

4) What is the title of the story?

____

5) Where did Anna perform lute?

____

Expressive language
Oral expression
Level 1

Unscramble and write the word to complete the sentence.

1. gyeren  Healthy food gives me __________.
2. stuifr  Bananas and apples are_________.
3. ymg  I like to exercise at the _________.
4. eelf regat  I ______________ today.
5. ssldaa  I like to have ________ for lunch.
6. nimsitav  Fruits a vegetables have lots of___________.
7. talbesvege  Eat your __________!
8. gnicora oodsf  ____________ are very healthy.
9. knuj ofdo 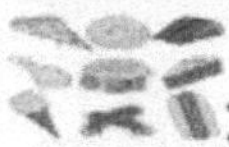 I used to eat lots of _________.
10. Leef yrghnu  I ___________. Let's eat!

Expressive language
Oral expression
Level 2

I help at home

Grammar.

Read the sentences and fill in the gaps with a pronoun, verb to be or a noun.

1 She is .... the mirror
2 He is taking out the ....
3 She is .... the floor
4 They .... washing up the dishes
5 .... is feeding the dog
6 He is .... the toilet
7 She is ....
8 He .... doing the laundry

Vocabulary.

Rearrange the letters to find out the word.

1 ROOMB ....

2 NAPTUDS ....

3 VENO ....

4 UUCMVA NEARCLE ....

Graphomotor skills
Assessment

Graphic motor skills are those skills necessary for a child to write successfully. poor grapho motor Skill is is a disconnect between a child's thought and his or her ability to write them down and Express it beautifully to the audience.

Students with graphic motor problems are frequently called lazy and motivated for your positional because they are reluctant to produce written work when demanded. many times these are the children who dislike the school and quit trying. children who have poor graph of motor function struggles with cutting food doing puzzles are menu plating small objects by hand. the child uses a pen grape that is strange or awkword is the sign of poor grapho Motor skills.

There are five individual skill areas associated with graph for Motor skills they are the following:-

visual perceptual skills- the ability to see a letter or a words and assign meaning for judge accuracy.

orthographic coding- the ability to store letters or group of letters in memory and then retrieve them when required.

kinesthetics feedback- the ability to know where a part of body is in space for the purpose of carrying out necessary motor movement.

motor planning and execution- this is the ability to carry out necessary motor movement and is also called praxis.

Visual motor coordination- the ability to correlate motor movement with visual perception is called visual motor coordination.

below is the sample of the class 4 child's writing who has graphic motor issues:-

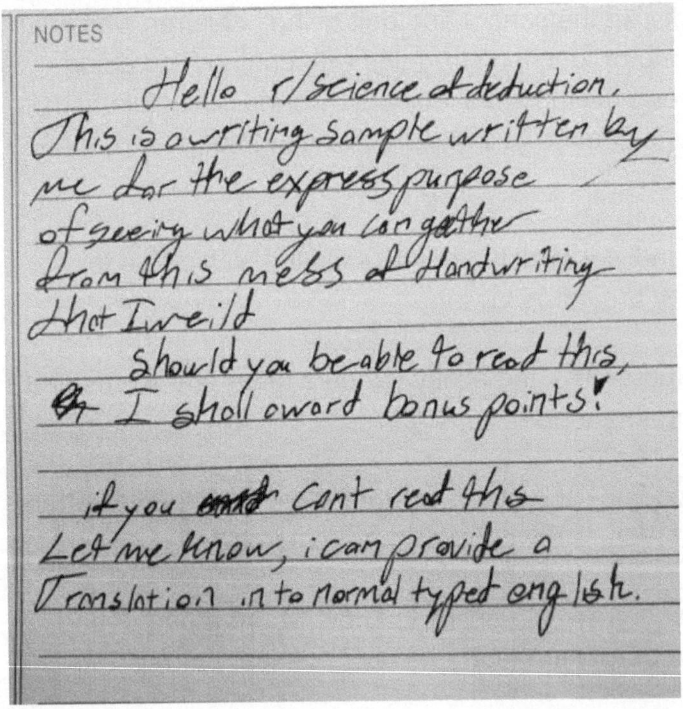
NOTES

Hello r/science of deduction,
This is a writing sample written by
me for the express purpose
of seeing what you can gather
from this mess of Handwriting
that I weild

Should you be able to read this,
I shall award bonus points!

if you cant read this
Let me know, i can provide a
Translation into normal typed english.

Grapho motor skill assessment

Children with poor graphic Motor skills usually rely on verbal communication to survive because written expression eludes them. while assessing the graphic Motor skills we have to to consider the following points carefully .

1. following are few prerequisite skill to handwriting which the observer should observe while giving the worksheet to the child.

- Scribbling
- identifying shapes
- recognising likeness and differences
- eye hand coordination
- cutting and pasting within the given space

2. observing the posture of the child:-

- child should say it in such posture that the back should erect all times.
- shoulder should be relaxed and slightly bent forward.
- head should not be too close to the paper.

3. paper position- for a right hand person land paper to the left is appropriate, Where are in for a left hand person client paper to the right is is appropriate.

Efficient pencil grasp

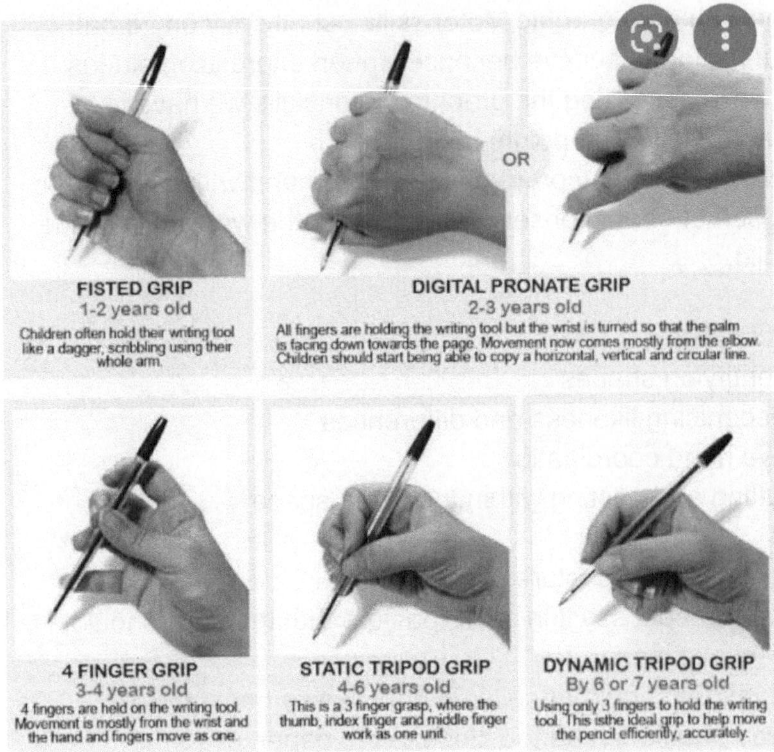

Mathematical assessment

Mathematical calculations are complex system of skills concepts and processes. the understanding acquisition and competence depends on the interaction of many abilities and cognitive mechanism. maths learning difficulties are common significant and worthy of serious instruction null and tension in both regular and special education classes. students may respond to repeated failure with withdrawal of effort lowered self-esteem and avoidance behaviour.

math learning problems range from mild to severe and manifest themselves in a variety of ways. most common are difficulties with efficient recall of basic arithmetic Fact and reliability in written computation. in sum, as a special educator there is much we can do and need to do in this area that Falls for so much greater attention than we have typically provided.

Math assessment
Level 1

Write the number name:		2. Write the number numeral:	
130		One hundred and thirty-two	
133		One hundred and thirty-four	
135		One hundred and thirty-six	

2. Complete the sums:

130 + 1 =	100 + = 133	130 + = 137	139 - 9 =
130 + 3 =	100 + = 134	130 + = 139	137 - 7 =
130 + 5 =	100 + = 136	130 + = 132	135 - 30 =

3. Fill in the missing numbers:

140		142		144					

4. Decompose (breaking up numbers)

+ + = 135	500+80+3 =	8+40+300=	+ + =364

5. Write the following numbers from smallest to biggest.

125	135	185	205	115	155	215	145	165	375

Math assessment
level 2

Describe, compare and arrange numbers.

1. Fill in the missing numbers. [9]

____; 233	299; ____; 301	150; ____
____; 176	124; ____; 126	366; ____
____; 350	282; ____; 284	215; ____

2. Order the numbers in descending order. [2]

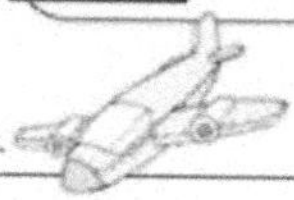

312; 123; 231	________; ________; ________.
236; 241; 243	________; ________; ________.

3. Arrange the series of numbers in ascending order. [2]

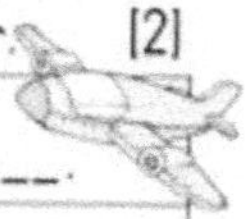

119; 291; 109	________; ________; ________.
256; 146; 386	________; ________; ________.

4. Complete the table. [4]

Double the numbers		Halve the numbers	
15→	24→	18→	50→

5. Complete: More / less than. [4]

5 more than 346 = _______	10 less than 174 = _______
4 less than 233 = _______	3 more than 378 = _______

Place value worksheet

Place value in maths.Describes the position or place of a digit in a number.Each dessert has a place in a number.When we represent the number in general form, the position of each digit will be expanded.Let's do the following worksheet and understand more.

Use your place value skills to count the total in each box.

① 500 + 30 + 2 Total = 532	② 600 + 60 + 9 Total = ____
③ 700 + 70 + 3 Total = ____	④ 200 + 10 + 4 Total = ____
⑤ 400 + 60 + 2 Total = ____	⑥ 100 + 10 + 1 Total = ____
⑦ 500 + 90 + 9 Total = ____	⑧ 300 + 30 + 2 Total = ____
⑨ 600 + 80 + 5 Total = ____	⑩ 800 + 10 + 1 Total = ____
⑪ 900 + 20 + 4 Total = ____	⑫ 700 + 50 + 2 Total = ____

Place value worksheet
Level 1

4 - Digit Place Value Worksheet

Write the 4-digit number based on the given place values

1. ______ = 2,000 + 400 + 70 + 3
2. ______ = 8,000 + 600 + 40 + 4
3. ______ = 6,000 + 900 + 50 + 1
4. ______ = 2,000 + 900 + 60 + 2
5. ______ = 9,000 + 60
6. ______ = 6,000 + 100 + 40
7. ______ = 7,000 + 500 + 80 + 9
8. ______ = 1,000 + 800 + 90 + 1
9. ______ = 5,000 + 600 + 60 + 6
10. ______ = 3,000 + 600 + 30 + 2
11. ______ = 4,000 + 800 + 90 + 2
12. ______ = 9,000 + 400 + 30 + 7
13. ______ = 9,000 + 700 + 60 + 5
14. ______ = 5,000 + 500 + 50 + 5
15. ______ = 6,000 + 100 + 40
16. ______ = 8,000 + 800 + 10 + 1
17. ______ = 2,000 + 200 + 5
18. ______ = 1,000 + 900 + 90 + 9

Place value worksheet
Level 2

5-Digit Place Value Worksheet

The 5-digit number 62755 can be expanded in the form 60000 + 2000 + 700 + 50 + 5. That is,

62755 = 60000 + 2000 + 700 + 50 + 5

Write the 5-digit number in the blank space given.

1. 40,000 + 300 + 7 = ____________
2. 90,000 + 6,000 + 60 + 4 = ____________
3. 30,000 + 5,000 + 700 + 60 + 1 = ____________
4. 40,000 + 8,000 + 600 + 60 + 4 = ____________
5. 90,000 + 5,000 + 300 + 80 + 2 = ____________

DIAGNOSTIC ARITHMETIC TEST
(MODIFIED FROM SCHONELL'S)

I. ADDITION

(a) 1 + 1 = (b) 1 + 3 = (c) 2 + 5 = (d) 8 + 3 = (e) 6 + 3 =

II. SUBTRACTION

(a) 3 - 2 = (b) 5 - 3 = (c) 11 - 6 = (d) 9 - 5 = (e) 13 - 8 =

III. MULTIPLICATION

(a) 1 x 3= (b) 2 x 0 = (c) 6 x 9 = (d) 8 x 5 = (e) 9 x 8 =

IV. DIVISION

(a) 2) 4 ((b) 5) 5 ((c) 4) 12 ((d) 3) 24 ((e) 6) 54 (

V. MISCELLANEOUS

(a) 3 + 8 = (b) 12 - 5 = (c) 7 x 6 = (d) 7) 42 (

VI. GRADED ADDITION

(a) 14 + 3 (b) 31 + 66 (c) 19 + 9 (d) 87 + 31 (e) 56 + 69

VII. GRADED SUBTRACTION

(a) 98 - 3 (b) 346 - 215 (c) 71 - 2 (d) 331 - 18 (e) 180 - 71

VIII. GRADED MULTIPLICATION

(a) 22 x 4 (b) 303 x 36 (c) 76 X 39 (d) 106 x 72 (e) 348 x 12

22x4 303 x 36 76 x 39 106 x 72 348 x 12

IX. GRADED DIVISION

(a) 4) 44 (b) 3) 906 (c) 4) 800 (d) 5) 1515 (e) 5) 156

X. ADDITION (FRACTIONS)

(a) $\frac{3}{7} + \frac{1}{3}$ (b) $7 + \frac{2}{3}$ (c) $\frac{5}{8} + \frac{1}{8} =$

XI. SUBTRACTION (FRACTIONS)

(a) $\frac{7}{9} + \frac{2}{9}$ (b) $2\frac{7}{11} - \frac{7}{11} =$ (c) $9\frac{5}{6} - 3\frac{7}{12} =$

XII. MULTIPLICATION (FRACTIONS)

(a) $\frac{3}{16} \times 5 =$ (b) $7 \times \frac{2}{7} =$ (c) $\frac{2}{5} \times \frac{3}{7} =$

XIII. DIVISION

(a) $8 \div \frac{5}{4} =$ (b) $\frac{1}{2} \div \frac{1}{3} =$ (c) $5\frac{3}{5} \div 4 =$

Adequate Means	Correct Answers		
at Ist Standard	I	=	3/5
	II	=	3/5
at II Standard	III	=	3/5
	IV	=	3/5
at III Standard	V	=	2/4
	VI	=	3/5
	VII	=	3/5
at IV Standard	VIII	=	3/5
	IX	=	3/5
at V Standard	X	=	2/3
	XI	=	2/3
	XII	=	2/3
	XIII	=	2/3

Logical and reasoning Worksheet
Level 1

Logical reasoning is a mental activity that aims to arrive at a conclusion in a rigorous manner.In the form of interferences.By starting from a set of premises and reasoning to a conclusion supported by these premises.

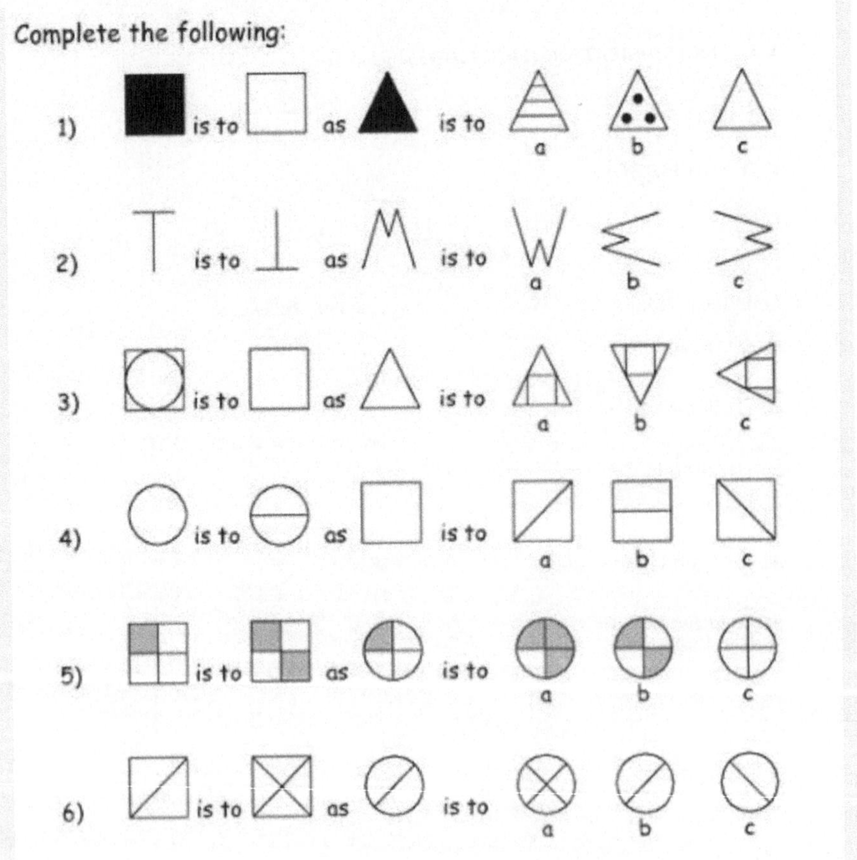

Logical and reasoning worksheet
Level 2

The blank square in the first five boxes needs to be filled by one of the patterns in the second five boxes. Circle the correct letter.

Example

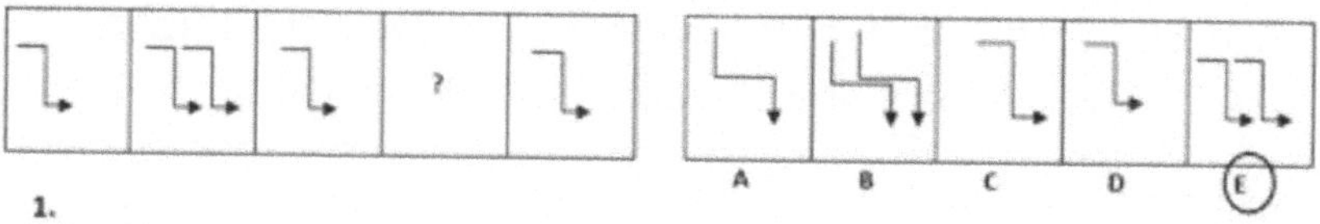

1.

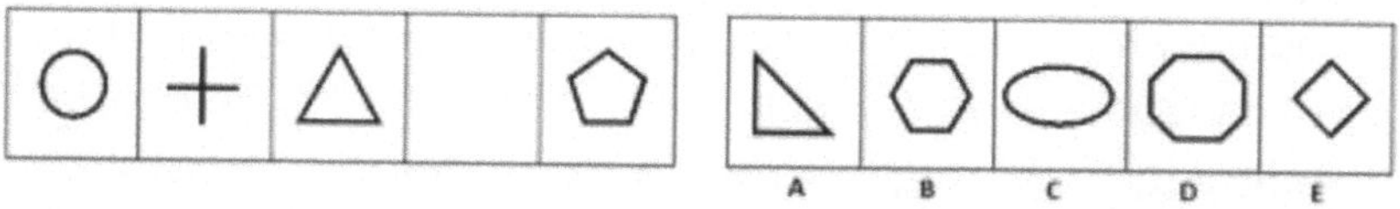

2.

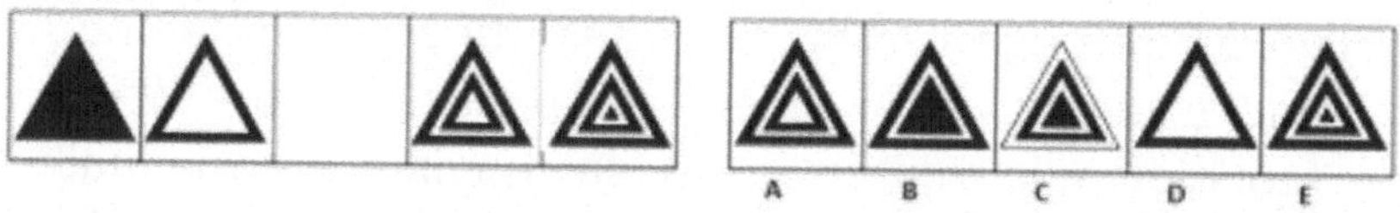

3.

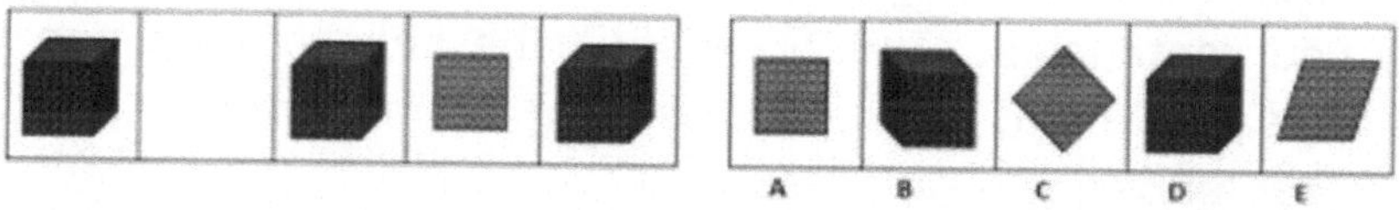

4.

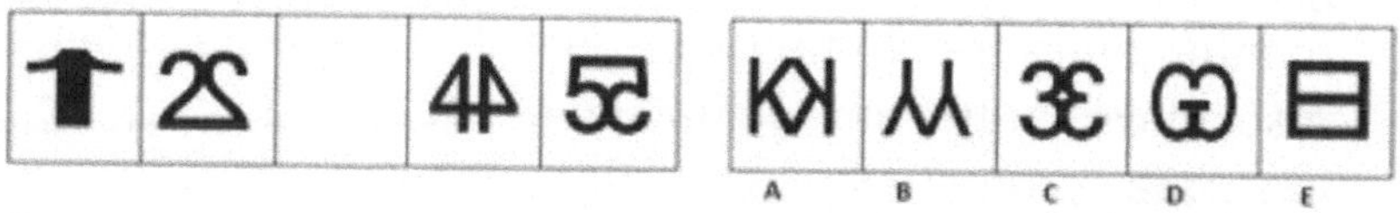

5.

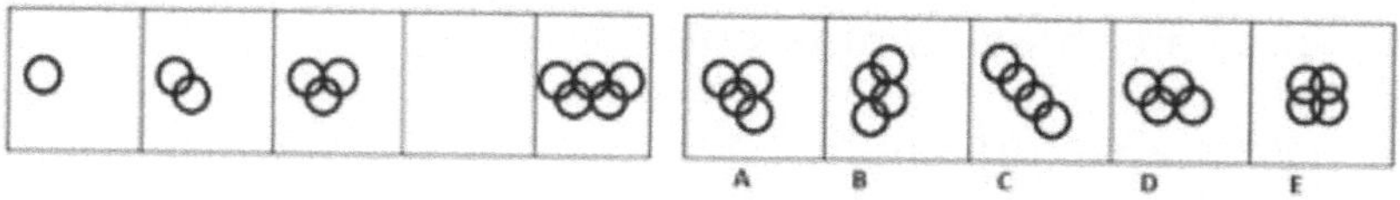

Remediation in Writing

Words are the primary means of communication for human beings. Using them is the way we tell one another what we want and what we don't want, what we think, and how we feel. When words are spoken, they are a wonderful asset-quick, direct, and easy. But when words must be written, they can become burdensome, part of a slow and laborious task.

Writing is the most sophisticated and complex achievement of the language system. In the sequence of language development, it is typically the last to be learned, although the early literacy approach encourages children to write even before they learn to read. Through writing, we integrate previous learning and experiences in listening, speaking, and reading. Proficiency in written language requires an adequate basis of oral language skills as well as many other competencies. The writer must be able to keep one idea in mind while formulating it into words and sentences and must be skilled in planning the correct graphic form for each letter and word while manipulating the writing instrument. The writer must also have sufficient visual and motor memory to integrate complex eye–hand relationships.

There are **three components of writing**:

- **Written expression**
- **Spelling**
- **Handwriting (graphomotor)**

Written Expression

Competent writing requires many related abilities, including facility in spoken language, the ability to read, skills in spelling, legible handwriting or skill with computer keyboarding, knowledge of the rules of written usage, and cognitive strategies for organizing and planning the writing.

The Writing Connection in the Integrated Language System

The links among the elements of language connect the language forms with one another and also strengthen the underlying language system. Extensive oral language experiences promote reading. Instruction in reading improves performance in writing. Experiences with writing and composing improve one's language and skill in speaking and reading. All strengthen the underlying language system (Richek et al., 2002).

By its very nature, writing is an active process. The physical aspect of writing literally forces active involvement from the writer. Writers perform the actions of picking up a pen or pencil (or keyboard) and recording their thoughts.

Early Literacy and Writing

The term *early literacy* refers to the child's early entrance into the world of words, language, and stories. The concept of early literacy emphasizes the interrelatedness of the various forms of language in the child's development. Children develop literacy through simultaneous experiences with oral language, reading, and writing.

The early literacy philosophy suggests that writing may emerge earlier than reading and may actually develop earlier than reading. Writing is a more self-involving activity than reading because the meaning of a writer's message originates from within the writer and is known to the writer in advance. In contrast, reading requires that the reader interpret someone else's ideas and use of language, which is a more difficult task for the beginner.

The Writing Process

There has been a major shift in instructional emphasis toward the *process* of writing rather than the *product* of writing. Writing is a learned skill that can be taught in a school setting as a thinking–learning activity, with emphasis on the writing process. As a cognitive process, writing requires both backward and forward thinking. Good writers do not simply sit down and produce a text. Rather, they move through several stages of the writing process-prewriting, writing a draft, revising, and sharing with an audience (Graves 1983, 1994).

Stage 1: Prewriting

During this first stage, the writer gathers ideas and refines them before beginning formal writing. Prewriting involves a type of brain-storming, such as talking through ideas, jotting notes in the margin, or developing a graphic organizer or list of main points. During this stage, the writer also identifies an intended audience. Students are more willing to write if they choose the topic. They may write about someone they know, an event, or themselves. Teachers can help by asking students to make a list of special people or to list things they did during a holiday break.

Stage 2: Writing a Draft

In this stage, the writer records ideas on paper. *Drafting* emphasizes that this is only one version of what may eventually be written, and it will be changed. The first draft is for the writer, not the reader. Writers jot down words, sentences, and paragraphs, which may lead to new ideas or ways to revise what is already written. At this stage, ideas may overflow, with little attention to organization or grammar.

Stage 3: Revising

After completing prewriting and drafting, the writer refines the text during revising. There may be several revisions, each involving different types of changes-content, expression of ideas, vocabulary, sentence structure, and sequence of ideas. The last revision is *editing*, which includes checking for grammatical, punctuation, and spelling errors. This stage requires a critical view of one's own work.

Stage 4: Sharing with an Audience

This stage is important because it gives value and purpose to the writing process. It offers students opportunities to receive feedback and to perceive themselves as authors responding to an audience. The writer considers the audience and determines how well the ideas are communicated. Sharing may take the form of a presentation, bulletin board display, or puppet show.

Principles for Teaching the Writing Process (Graham et al., 2001)

1. During prewriting, the writing process needs time, input, and attention. Writers need something to write about. Prior experiences stimulate ideas. Assigning a writing task without prewriting preparation will not produce a quality written product. Teachers should provide input experiences such as trips, discussions, stories, art, films, and internet searches.

2. Drafting frees students from over-focusing on mechanics. All writers make mistakes in spelling and grammar in first drafts. These need not be corrected immediately. The student should focus on ideas first.

3. Revising helps students edit their work. Many students think writing is complete once a first draft is done. Teachers can model that writing always needs editing by showing their own initial drafts.

4. Avoid excessive corrections. Heavy red-ink corrections discourage students from expressing ideas. Negative reinforcement leads students to use only simple words they can spell correctly, limiting creativity.

A Learning Strategy Approach to Teaching Writing

A structured approach known as *Self-Regulated Strategy Development (SRSD)* is recommended for teaching writing. The six stages of the SRSD model are:

1. Develop background knowledge
2. Discuss it (including a writing strategy)
3. Model it (thinking aloud)
4. Memorize it
5. Support it
6. Independent performance

Strategies for Writing

A variety of strategies help students generate ideas, share them, use descriptive vocabulary, and make writing purposeful.

- **Writing conversations:** Two students converse through writing only.
- **Personal journals:** Students record personal events or reflections.
- **Patterned writing:** Students use predictable books and write their own version.
- **Graphic organizers:** Visual displays that structure ideas and concepts, improving comprehension. Common organizers include Venn diagrams.
- **Drawing pictures:** Helps students express ideas.
- **Computer and word processing**

Handwriting

There are three commonly taught ways to produce writing:

- **Manuscript writing** (a form of printing)
- **Cursive writing** (script)
- **Keyboarding** (typing)

Even with increasing computer use, handwriting remains an essential skill. It is concrete and provides a permanent record. Handwriting depends on visual perception, visual-motor coordination, fine motor control, and memory for letter forms.

Manuscript Writing

Introduced in kindergarten, manuscript writing uses letters composed of circles and straight lines, which are close to printed forms.

Cursive Writing

Cursive letters are connected. Students typically transition to cursive in grade 3, though some schools introduce it as late as grade 5. Cursive minimizes spatial judgment problems and reduces letter reversals common in manuscript writing.

The Left-Handed Student

Left-handed writers often face challenges because writing from left to right may obscure what they have written. Left-handedness is natural, and students who prefer using the left hand should be allowed to do so.

Keyboarding

Keyboarding is motorically easier and produces more legible output. Learning to type is demanding and requires regular instruction, drill, and practice.

Graphomotor Function

Writing involves fine motor and graphomotor skills. A person may have excellent fine-motor skills while still struggling with graphomotor functions specific to writing.

Writing is among the most complex activities for students. The motor components of writing are intricate and highly demanding, especially in cursive writing.

Four Components of Graphomotor Function

- **Pre-visualization**
- **Graphomotor memory**
- **Graphomotor production**
- **Graphomotor feedback**

1. **Pre-visualization** – Imagining a letter or number before writing it

• Students with strong pre-visualization write smoothly with consistent formation and proper spacing.

• Students with weak pre-visualization write with reduced legibility and leave inconsistent spacing.

2. **Graphomotor Memory** – Recalling letter and number forms

• Students with strong memory write quickly and consistently.

• Students with weak memory struggle with each letter, producing slow, effortful writing with frequent erasures and preference for printing.

3. **Graphomotor Production** – Executing the motor actions of writing

• Students with strong production use a normal tripod grasp and form letters easily.

• Students with weak production drop writing utensils, write slowly, or use immature grips (e.g., fist-like grip).

4. **Graphomotor Feedback** – Knowing where the writing utensil is during formation

• Students with strong feedback write without close visual monitoring and apply correct pressure.

• Students with weak feedback keep their eyes close to the page, use wrist and elbow instead of small-muscle control, apply excessive pressure, and wear down pencil points. They often need frequent breaks or sharpening.

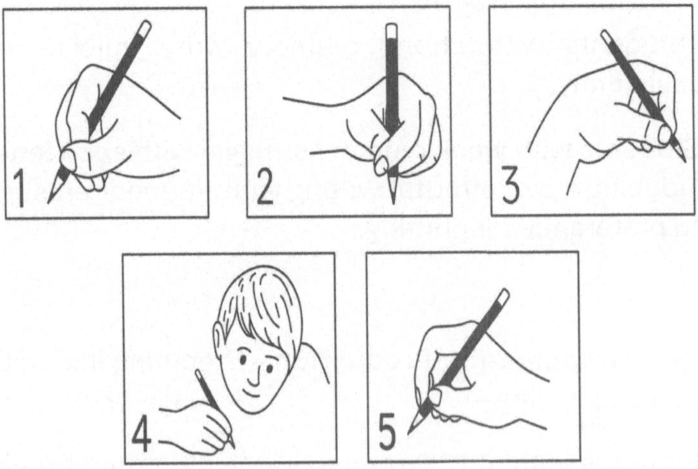

In drawing 1, the student is immobilizing the second and third fingers by placing the thumb across the joints and using mainly wrist movements for implementation and feedback. This grip is commonly associated with finger agnosia.

In drawing 2, the pencil is held perpendicular to the page. The second finger, which ordinarily stabilizes the pencil, is not doing so. Thus, an excessive number of joints are mobile during writing. This grip is found in some students with fine motor dyspraxia.

In drawing 3, note the left-handed hook with the pencil held too tightly (not the hyperextended distal joint of the second finger).

In drawing 4, the grip is distal, and the student is over-relying on close visual monitoring of the pencil movements. This student may have difficulty appreciating nonvisual feedback during writing.

In drawing 5, in a normal tripod grip, the thumb and middle finger effect most of the movement at their middle joints while the forefinger regulates the pressure. The pencil is held at a forty-five degree angle to the page.

REMEDIATION IN LANGUAGE

Linguistics and Language Learning

Linguistics is the systematic study of language and its nature, development, function, and use. Linguistic concepts have implications for every form of language: listening, speaking, reading, writing, spelling, grammar, and usage.

The Linguistic System

We need to understand several basic linguistic concepts and terms to discuss the linguistic system. These include phonology, morphology, syntax, semantics, and pragmatics.

Phonology

The phonological linguistic system refers to the speech sounds in a language. The smallest unit of sound is a *phoneme*, a sound that cannot be broken down further.

Example: In the word *cat*, there are three phonemes: /c/ /a/ /t/.

In the word *high*, there are two phonemes: /h/ /igh/.

Phonemic recognition is essential for learning to read as well as for oral language. *Phonics* is the recognition, analysis, and synthesis of phoneme elements in written words.

Morphology

The morphological linguistic system refers to the meaning units in language. The smallest unit of meaning is a *morpheme*.

Examples:

book → 1 morpheme

books → 2 morphemes (book + s), where *s* indicates plurality.

Children who are unaware of exceptions to morphemic rules may overgeneralize:

Example: fight → *fighted*, go → *goed*.

Syntax

The linguistic system of syntax is the grammar system of a language-the way words are strung together to form sentences. A child with a syntactic language disorder may not have learned how to order words correctly.

Semantics

The linguistic system of semantics is vocabulary or word meaning.

Pupils with limited vocabulary or difficulty relating words to meaningful ideas may have a semantic language disorder. Vocabulary development continues throughout life.

Pragmatics

The linguistic system of pragmatics relates to the social use of language-how a speaker uses language in context. Pragmatics considers:

- the relationship between speaker and listener
- the speaker's assessment of the listener's background knowledge
- turn-taking in conversations
- staying on topic
- asking relevant questions
- eye contact, appearance, and engagement

Forms of the Language System

The language system encompasses listening, speaking, reading, and writing. Acquisition follows a developmental sequence:

1. Listening
2. Speaking
3. Reading

4. Writing

Listening and speaking develop first as oral skills and are part of the primary language system. Reading and writing are secondary because they involve symbols of spoken language.

Two forms are input or receptive (listening and reading), and two are output or expressive (speaking and writing).

Listening and reading involve receiving information. Speaking and writing involve generating ideas from the brain and sending them outward.

Language as a Communication Process

Language allows people to communicate. Other methods include gestures, body language, and sign language. Communication involves sending a message (expressive language) and receiving a message (receptive language). A breakdown can occur at any point.

Examples:

- In expressive language, impairment may occur when forming ideas, coding them into spoken or written symbols, or recalling sequences of language.
- In receptive language, impairment may occur when receiving or perceiving symbols through

the eye or ear or in integrating these stimuli in the brain or memory.

Dr. Mel Levine on Language

Language is all-consuming in students' lives. It is essential for daily communication and is the main ingredient of reading, spelling, and writing proficiency. Language connects closely with memory because linguistic meaning is stored in long-term memory (LTM) and active working memory (AWM). It is necessary for forming concepts, self-coaching, self-control, and interacting smoothly with others.

Levels of Language

Language professionals commonly identify seven levels of language processing-five major ones are shown in the table below, with corresponding neurodevelopmental functions:

LEVELS OF LANGUAGE PROCESSING

Corresponding and Production	**Neurodevelopmental Functions**
Phonology: Appreciation of individual sound units and sound sequences, and the capacity to discriminate sounds.	Phonological Processing
Morphology: System of rules for combining units of meaning (morphemes) to convey ideas (e.g., prefixes, suffixes, roots).	Morphological Sense
Semantics: Knowledge of words and meanings.	Semantic Understanding, Semantic Use, Word Retrieval
Syntax: Combining words to form meaningful sentences according to grammar rules.	Comprehension and Sentence Formulation
Discourse: Language that extends beyond sentences (e.g., passages, paragraphs).	Discourse Processing, Discourse Production, Verbal Elaboration

Each level includes both receptive (processing incoming information) and expressive (producing outgoing information) components. Students may have strong receptive language and weak expressive language, or vice versa.

Example: A student may understand what is being said (receptive) but be unable to form meaningful sentences (expressive).

The Two Additional Language Levels Are:

- **Pragmatics:** Social language use; part of social cognition.
- **Metalinguistics:** The ability to reflect on language and understand how it works.

Higher Language Functioning in Early Adolescence

Early adolescents often struggle with the higher-level language needed for academic success. Students need language:

- as a learning tool
- to enhance memory and organization
- for problem solving
- for concept formation
- for abstract, inferential, and symbolic thinking
- for complex, dense, and extensive reading and writing

Cultural Considerations in Language Functioning in School

Some students struggle with classroom language demands because their cultural experiences differ from the expectations of the school environment.

Examples:

- In some cultures, asking questions such as "Who? What? Why?" may be considered inappropriate.
- The closer students' home language experiences are to school expectations, the better their academic success.

It is important to validate students' cultural language experiences while also strengthening classroom language skills to support success.

RECEPTIVE LANGUAGE

Receptive Language refers to processing and understanding incoming oral and written information.

In many school settings, learning depends heavily on language for transmitting knowledge.

Receptive Language facilitates:

- the ability to follow directions
- the understanding of questions
- the processing of verbal explanations
- the comprehension of literate/decontextualized language used in the classroom and in texts
- the ability to determine important details when reading
- reading skills that reflect adequate decoding and comprehension

Language processing (Receptive Language) occurs at multiple levels, including sounds (phonemes), basic units of meaning (morphemes), word-level meanings (semantics), sentence structure and grammar (syntax), paragraph and passage organization (discourse), social aspects of language (pragmatics), and language monitoring and reflection (metalinguistics).

Students may show Receptive Language weaknesses at one or more of these levels. Weaknesses may lead to difficulty following directions or understanding explanations, poor reading comprehension, limited understanding of subtle language features, and lack of awareness of their own comprehension.

Students with Receptive Language weaknesses often have difficulty with attention in environments where language is complex and decontextualized, such as school. At home, language may be more predictable and familiar, making these weaknesses less apparent. Difficulties are especially noticeable during tasks requiring sustained listening. These students often perform better with visual–spatial tasks than with linguistic ones.

Five Components of Receptive Language

1. **Phonological Processing**
2. **Morphological Sense**
3. **Semantic Understanding**
4. **Sentence Comprehension**
5. **Discourse Processing**

1. Phonological Processing - Receiving, distinguishing, and manipulating the sounds in words

Students with strong Phonological Processing can identify individual sounds, break words into phonemes, hold sounds in Active Working Memory, and blend them. They retrieve words easily, appreciate rhyming and alliteration, and recognize sound patterns.

Students with weak Phonological Processing often struggle with decoding skills. They may have difficulty with coarticulated language sounds (sounds blending together) and elusive stop consonants such as /k/ and /t/. Even mild phonological gaps can make learning a second language difficult. Everyday dialect features may also cause phonological challenges.

Weak phonological skills affect Expressive Language as well. Students may struggle with articulating sounds and spelling words accurately.

2. Morphological Sense - interpreting parts of words that convey meaning

Students with strong Morphological Sense understand how prefixes, suffixes, and root words function. They interpret inflections and intonations and recognize letter patterns.

Students with weak Morphological Sense struggle to recognize misspelled words, especially when unaware of morphemes such as *pre*, *re*, *ed*. Vocabulary acquisition suffers when students fail to notice meaningful word parts (e.g., *preview* vs. *review*). They may have difficulty with verb tenses, plurals, and possessives.

Weak Morphological Sense also affects expressive language. Students may misuse inflections and have spelling difficulties because they fail to use meaningful letter patterns.

3. Semantic Understanding - knowing the meanings of words

Students with strong Semantic Understanding quickly learn new vocabulary and respond accurately to questions using new terminology. They build semantic networks and understand technical vocabulary used in academic subjects.

Students with weak Semantic Understanding struggle to grasp new terms. Their vocabulary may be rigid, superficial, or overly literal. They may have difficulty with figurative language, symbolic meanings, or words with multiple definitions. Weak semantic skills particularly affect reading comprehension in middle school, where students must learn and use complex vocabulary.

Foreign language learning can be especially challenging for these students.

4. Sentence Comprehension - Understanding sentences and sentence structure

Students with strong Sentence Comprehension follow directions, understand explanations, and interpret higher-level language (e.g., proverbs, humor, figurative language, ambiguities, inferences). They grasp grammar rules, read well, and handle word problems in math.

Students with weak Sentence Comprehension may struggle with complex sentences, misunderstand questions (especially "wh-" questions), and rely on ineffective strategies such as focusing on the order of mention or personal experience. They may have slow sentence-processing speed and difficulty activating prior knowledge quickly enough.

5. Discourse Processing - interpreting language beyond sentence boundaries

Students with strong Discourse Processing maintain interest during oral presentations or long passages. They use Active Working Memory to process and retain information, comprehend logical sequences, and understand cause-and-effect relationships.

Students with weak Discourse Processing often need repetition or summaries. They may struggle with text-heavy classes and be confused by conventions such as:

- **anaphora** - meaning depends on a previous sentence
- **cataphora** - meaning depends on a following sentence

Common Indicators of Possible Receptive Language Weaknesses

- Difficulty following directions (e.g., looking around to copy what others are doing)
- Confusion when processing verbal explanations (needs frequent repetition)
- Difficulty with spoken language requiring rapid processing and retrieval
- Strength in everyday conversational language but difficulty with academic language
- Delayed reading, spelling, and writing acquisition despite strengths in arithmetic (except word problems)
- Problems arise depending on which aspects of language (phonology, semantics, syntax) are weak
- Difficulty handling multiple simultaneous language demands
- Trouble recognizing key information when reading
- Attention problems in school
- Possible behavior problems at home and school

Expressive Language

Expressive Language refers to communicating and producing ideas orally and in writing.

Language production is an integral part of most school activities. Proficient language production involves multiple levels of functioning, including sounds and basic units (phonology and morphology), word meanings (semantics), sentence word order (syntax), paragraph and passage organization (discourse), social applications (pragmatics), and language monitoring and reflection (metalinguistics).

Language facilitates the ability to:

- formulate and express an opinion
- use technical/contextualized vocabulary
- be elaborative in school
- revise something that has been said (e.g., strong communication-repair skills)
- make and keep friends
- resolve conflict without resorting to violence

Students with poor language production have difficulty relating to others and demonstrating their knowledge and skills. They may show hesitant or labored verbal expression, low ideational density (few ideas), trouble organizing ideas, and overuse of high-frequency vocabulary (common words lacking richness). These students may also exhibit performance anxiety, aggressive or avoidant behaviors related to language tasks, and difficulty meeting language demands in writing and social situations.

Six Components of Expressive Language

1. **Articulation and Fluency**
2. **Semantic Use**
3. **Word Retrieval**
4. **Sentence Formulation**
5. **Discourse Production**
6. **Verbal Elaboration**

1. Articulation and Fluency - Using mouth muscles effectively to generate smooth and intelligible speech

- Students with strong Articulation and Fluency can pronounce words clearly and speak without hesitation. They perform tongue twisters with ease.
- Students with weak Articulation and Fluency have hesitant or labored speech patterns and are often hard to understand.

2. Semantic Use - Properly utilizing word meanings

- Students with strong Semantic Use apply newly learned terms appropriately, including abstract, symbolic, and figurative language (e.g., idioms). They use multiple meanings of words depending on context (e.g., "I saw a seal at the zoo," "I will seal the envelope").
- Students with weak Semantic Use confuse similar words, show impoverished vocabulary, seldom use new terms independently, and rely on primitive associations (e.g., dog/bite). Their speech or writing may contain incorrect word usage and excessive literalness.

3. Word Retrieval - Finding the right words quickly and easily

- Students with strong Word Retrieval produce specific words without hesitation and excel in impromptu speaking.
- Students with weak Word Retrieval experience the "tip-of-the-tongue" phenomenon, hesitate frequently, overuse fillers ("uh," "whatchamacallit"), or substitute definitions for words they cannot recall (e.g., "the thing that horses go around on" for *merry-go-round*).

4. Sentence Formulation - Expressing thoughts in complete sentences

- Students with strong Sentence Formulation use grammatically correct sentences, vary structure, and write or speak with cohesion. They create complex sentences using conjunctions, clauses, and correct pronoun use.
- Students with weak Sentence Formulation rely on simple declarative sentences, struggle with rate of production, and respond slowly. They often misuse humor or indirect meaning, write sentence fragments or run-ons, omit words and endings, and make punctuation/capitalization errors. These difficulties often lead to spelling problems and weak written expression.

5. Discourse Production - Communicating information in a cohesive chain of sentences

- Students with strong Discourse Production explain ideas at length in an organized and logical sequence. They write essays and give oral presentations effectively.
- Students with weak Discourse Production produce sparse, underdeveloped compositions. They have difficulty summarizing, distinguishing important from unimportant content, and clarifying ideas for audiences.

6. Verbal Elaboration - Extending and developing ideas through language

- Students with strong Verbal Elaboration expand ideas with appropriate detail, description, and examples. They form and support arguments, incorporate figurative language, and integrate personal experience.
- Students with weak Verbal Elaboration give short or incomplete responses, repeat ideas, and fail to clarify or extend thoughts. They struggle with figurative language and critical analysis in oral presentations or writing.

Common Indicators of Possible Expressive Language Weaknesses

- Difficulty expressing ideas verbally or in writing
- Labored language expression (working harder than peers to express ideas)
- Hesitation and prolonged word-finding struggles
- Use of imprecise words or substituted definitions
- Difficulty revising or repairing communication
- Overreliance on circumlocutions (e.g., vague words like "thing," "stuff," "you know") and stalling behaviors

- Difficulty understanding the listener's perspective
- Lack of cohesive ties linking sentences smoothly
- Limited vocabulary growth and reliance on only high-frequency words

Spelling

Difficulties with Spelling

Spelling requires auditory and visual discrimination, sequence memory, analysis, synthesis, and integration-often simultaneously. Children with LD typically struggle with spelling because it requires producing a correct sequence of letters. Reading involves recognizing symbols already present on a page; recognition is easier than recall and production.

Good spellers master effective strategies and apply them consistently.

A strong spelling program uses **phonetic**, **rule-based**, and **morphemic** strategies.

1. Phonetic Spelling Strategies

The student listens for each sound in a word and attempts to represent those sounds with letters or letter combinations.

Instruction includes:

- basic spelling rules
- common phonograms

2. Rule-Based Spelling Strategies

Spelling must also follow the rules and generalizations of the language.

Example:

If a student knows the *ch* sound is spelled **tch** after a short vowel, they can spell *kitchen* correctly.

Chin Drops Method (for syllabification)

Place two fingers under your chin. Say the word slowly. Each time your chin drops, you've spoken a syllable. This helps determine where to break words for spelling.

3. Morphemic Spelling Strategies

These strategies rely on understanding how a word's meaning affects its spelling.

Instruction may include:

- Greek and Latin roots
- adding prefixes and suffixes to base words
- forming compound words
- abbreviations

As students mature, these strategies become automatic.

Word Sorts

Word sort example for ch, th, and sh digraphs

CH	TH	SH

Word Builder

Examples for building words using root, prefix, and suffix.

PREFIX	WORD	SUFFIX	NEW WORD	MEANING
Anti-	Social		Antisocial	Not social
	Taste	-ful	Tasteful	Full of taste
Mis-	Behave		Misbehave	Bad behavior
	happy	-ness	Happiness	Being happy
Super-	Natural		Supernatural	Above natural
	Fear	-less	Fearless	Without fear

Word Wall

High frequency words (example)

Table 1 – Word Wall

Aa	Bb	Cc	Dd	Ee	Ff	Gg	Hh
After	Best	Caug ht	Did	Eac h	First	Goo d	Him
Abou t	Bloc k	Can	Dow n	Eat	Fro m	Go	Hous e

Aa	Bb	Cc	Dd	Ee	Ff	Gg	Hh
All	Boy	Come	Drink			Get	Has
Ii	**Jj**	**Kk**	**Ll**	**Mm**	**Nn**	**Oo**	**Pp**
If	Jump	Know	Little	Many	New	On	Place
Into	Just		Like	More	Not	One	People
It's			Look	My	Night	Other	Put
Qq	**Rr**	**Ss**	**Tt**	**Uu**	**Vv**	**Ww**	**Xx**
Quiet	Run	Stop	There	Up	Very	Way	X-ray
Queen	Right	Set	Their	Us		Won't	
	Rain	Saw	That	Use		Was	
Yy				**Zz**			
You				Zoo			

Process for Learning New Words

Look

Say

Spell

Cover

Write

Check ✓

Tricky Words

Some common words are tricky to spell.

Quite often only **part** of the word gives us problems.

For example: **PEOPLE**

Can you think which parts of this spelling are easy or tricky?

What did you think?

- In the word *people* we have some letters that we don't hear when we say the word.
- • This can sometimes make words tricky.

pe o pl e

(Not heard)

Try saying these unstressed sounds as you say the word.

Look at the word shape.

(Representing the boxes for: little, where, you, are)

1. □□□□□ (little)
2. □□□□□ (where)

3. □ □ (you)
4. □ □ □ (are)

Mnemonics

A fun way to help children remember a set of tricky sight words visually and auditorily.

Examples

because

Big

Elephants

Can

Always

Understand

Small

Elephants

island

An island **is land** surrounded by water

necessary

1 collar

2 sleeves

= **necessary**

friend

A real **friend** is there to the **end**

piece

A piece of **pie**

secretary

A good **secretary** can keep a **secret**

business

Going by **bus** is good **business**

quiet

Keep **quiet**

about my **diet**

–ould words

Could

Should

Would

O U Little Devil

laugh

Laugh

And

U

Get

Happy

soldier

Soldiers sometimes **die** in battle

height & weight

There is an **eight** in **height** and **weight**

MNEMONICS – BRAINTRICKS

1. PIEce of PIE

2. There is a LIE in beLIEve

3. Wherever there's a Q there is U too

4. BECAUSE – Bunnies Eat Carrots And Uncle Sam's Eggs

5. WEDNESDAY – WED-NES-DAY
6. FRIEND – Fri the End
7. KNIFE – k-nif-e
8. Was – Wally and Sam
9. Website – Where the spider sits
10. Teacher – There is an ACHE in every teacher

Finally...

- The effectiveness of any reading and spelling exercise will be visible when prior planning has taken place.
- The reading exercise needs to be seen as a break-up of tasks (task analysis) so the child gets reinforcement of known skills and learns new skills needed to complete the task.
- Keep the interest of the child in mind.
- Keep your approach multisensory to ensure that the child is engaged.
- Use resources like pictures, internet, labels, cutouts, highlighters, and graphic organizers to make the exercise fun learning.

Reading Strategies

Why is reading important?

- It helps us make sense of the world around us.
- We read to gather and pick up information.
- We read to be able to function in our everyday lives.
- We read to communicate with others.
- We read for pleasure.

Reading Problems Noted Among Students with LD

- **Over dependency:** Students show an over-dependency on others for direction in their learning. Hence, individual assignments become difficult.
- **Difficulty Monitoring Performance:** Students are unable to monitor their own understanding of reading material.
- **Failure to Modify Strategies:** Strategies needed to read different types of text vary. Students with LD find it difficult to modify their strategies.
- **Memory Problems:** Students with LD demonstrate many memory problems and have lower possibilities of retaining understanding from reading material.

- **Difficulty Mastering Letter Sounds and Vocabulary:** Students with LD have difficulty learning letter sounds, combinations of sounds, and vocabulary words.
- **Difficulty in Generalization:** These students fail to transfer concepts learned in one context to another.
- **Difficulty in Approaching a Task Positively:** Due to repeated failures, students with LD often display less than positive attitudes towards challenging tasks.

Conceptualization of Reading Skills

For a general person, if asked to describe reading, they may say it means extracting meaning from words written on a page. As professionals, we know that this is overly simplistic. Even to reach this stage, there are several other stages we must master as readers.

We will be looking at **four different aspects of reading** and their **subskills**.

WORD ATTACK SKILLS

Word recognition or word attack skills deal with the ability to recognize and pronounce words.

- Phonics
- Sight words

• Combination Approach – Context clues and structural analysis

PHONICS

- Phonics refers to the relationship between printed letters (**graphemes**) and the sounds (**phonemes**) in language.
- Children must learn to **decode** printed language, translate print into sounds, and learn the alphabetic principle of the sound–symbol relationship.
- A precursor to learning phonics is **phonological awareness** – the recognition that speech can be segmented into phonemic units.
- Research supports that systematic phonic instruction contributes greatly to children's reading growth.
- Systematic phonics is effective when taught in Kindergarten.
- Phonics instruction helps prevent reading difficulties among at-risk students and helps remediate reading difficulties in students with reading disabilities.

A REVIEW OF COMMON PHONIC GENERALIZATIONS

The three aspects needed to understand when teaching or learning phonics are:

- Consonants
- Vowels
- Syllabication

Consonants

- Consonants are letters that are not vowels. Consonant sounds are formed by modifying or obstructing vocal sound with the organs of speech.
- Consonant sounds are relatively consistent and have a regular grapheme–phoneme relationship.
- Consonants include: **b, d, f, h, j, k, l, m, n, p, r, s, t, v, w, y** (initial position)

Consonants c and g

- **Hard c**: pronounced like *k* when followed by **a, o, u** (cat, cot, cup)
- **Soft c**: pronounced like *s* when followed by **i, e, y** (city, cent, cyber)
- **Hard g**: when followed by **a, o, u** (gas, go, gum)

- **Soft g**: when followed by **i, e, y**; sounds like *j* (gentle, gypsy, giraffe)

Consonant Blends

A consonant blend is a combination of two or three consonants blended so that each keeps its own identity.

s blends: sc, sk, sl, sw, sn, sp, sm, spl, spr, str

l blends: bl, cl, fl, gl, pl, sl

r blends: br, cr, dr, fr, gr, pr, tr

w blends: tw, dw

n blends: ng, nk

Consonant Digraphs

A consonant digraph is a combination of two consonant letters representing one phoneme or sound (not a blend).

Digraph	Examples
sh	ship, sheep, bush, wish
ch	chop, chill, bench, lunch
wh	wheel, whip
-ck	back, lick, lock, truck, deck
ph	phonics, phone, graph

Digraph	Examples
th	thin, bath

Silent Consonants

Silent consonants are consonants that, when combined with certain letters, are not pronounced.

Examples (silent letter in brackets):

- i (gh) – sight, light
- m (b) – comb, lamb
- (w) r – write, wrong
- (l) k – walk, talk
- (k) n – knee, know
- s (t) – listen
- f (t) – often, soften
- (g) n – gnat, gnome

Vowels

- The vowels are: **a, e, i, o, u** and sometimes **y**.
- **Short vowels**: a, e, i, o, u (sometimes y). A single vowel in the medial position usually has the short vowel sound (as in CVC words).

Short vowel sounds

- short a – *apple*
- short e – *egg*
- short i – *igloo*
- short o – *orange*
- short u – *umbrella*
- short y – as in *gypsy* (y has a short i sound)

Long vowels

- Long vowels: a, e, i, o, u (sometimes y)
- The long vowel sounds match the alphabet letter name.
- Various phonic rules help determine when vowels give long sounds.
- Some examples are: go, cake, eel, ice, no, uniform, April, cry

Double Vowels: Vowel Digraph

- Frequently, when two vowels appear together, the first vowel has the long sound while the second vowel is silent.
- This holds true for about 45% of the time.

- Examples: goat, tie, rain, eat, pay, bruise

Final e / Magic e

- In words with a vowel–consonant–e pattern (**VCe**), the vowel frequently has the long sound and the **e** is silent.
- Research shows this pattern appears in almost 60% of cases.
- Many words acquired by children by Grade 3 belong to the Magic e category.

Examples

made, pane, plate, cake, lake, hate

Pete, eke

mine, fine, hike, like, mile, slide, stripe

note, mode, dope, cone, more

cute, tube, flute, mule

Vowels Modified by r

- Vowels followed by the letter **r** are neither long nor short but are modified by the r-controlled pattern.

- This generalization holds true about 85% of the time.

Examples

star, her, stir, horn, fur

Diphthongs

- A diphthong consists of two adjacent printed symbols representing two vowels, each contributing to a blended speech sound.

Examples

joy, toil, cow, house, few

Syllabication

Number of Syllables

- There are as many syllables in a word as there are vowel sounds heard.
- Words may be monosyllabic or multisyllabic.
- *high, bat, made, kill* have 1 syllable
- *carpet, contact, letter* have 2 syllables
- *beautiful, natural* have 3 syllables
- *caterpillar, concentration* have 4 syllables
- *generalization* has 5 syllables

Sight Words

- Sight words are words recognized instantly, without hesitation or further analysis.
- Fluent reading requires most of the words in a selection to be sight words.
- Many graded lists of sight words exist, typically including 250–300 words a child should know by the end of third grade.
- One of the most natural ways to learn sight words is by reading stories.
- Another way to expose children to sight words is through language-experience stories.

Word Comprehension

• The ability to pronounce a word does not necessarily indicate the ability to understand its meaning.

• Understanding word meaning is referred to as *semantics*.

• Studies show that children recognize a word better in context than in isolation; therefore, contextual clues should be encouraged.

• Structural analysis refers to recognizing words through analysis of meaningful units such as prefixes, suffixes, root words, compound words (*airport*), contractions (*can't*), and word endings (plurals, *–ed, –er, –est, –ing*).

Strategies for Improving Reading Fluency

• **Repeated Reading:** The student rereads a short selection until a certain level of word-identification accuracy and fluency is reached.

• **Neurological Impress Method:** A read-along strategy in which the teacher and student read a passage together orally.

• **Paired Reading:** Two students read in pairs, alternating lines or pages, providing extensive reading practice.

- **Echo Reading:** The teacher models an oral reading passage, and the student imitates it.

Sentence Comprehension

- Read the following sentence:

Tina and Mona are classmates, Mona helps Tina with her craft work as she cannot hold the scissors well.

- Comprehending this sentence requires understanding the relationships between the words.

- Syntax refers to the relationships between words in sentences.

- In compound sentences like this, the reader must understand relationships such as pronouns, direct objects, and indirect objects.

Comprehension of Longer Texts

- Comprehension is the essence of the reading act.

- Along with word recognition, children must understand and interact with the text.

- Various comprehension strategies exist; some suit all ages, while others are specific to primary or secondary learners.

Activating Background Knowledge

• These strategies alert students to the background knowledge needed for comprehension and help build on prior experiences.

• They help the child connect to the text.

• **The Language Experience Method**

• **The K-W-L Technique**

a) The Language Experience Method

• This LEA is well accepted as a method that builds on the student's knowledge and language base.

• It links the different forms of language–listening, speaking, reading and writing.

• It uses the student's own experiences and language as the raw material.

• The student begins by dictating stories or narrating the experience of something like a nature walk, a birthday party or so.

• These stories then become the basis of their reading instruction.

• There is no predetermined rigid control over vocabulary, syntax or content.

• The teacher uses the text or the stories that the students compose to develop reading skills.

• The method is effective both in the beginning-to-read stage with young children and in corrective instruction with older students.

• The interest of the student is high as the reading is based on something the student has experienced and the language used is their natural language for expressing.

b) The K-W-L Technique

• It can be used for reading and studying content area textbooks or passages based on information topics.

• **K: What I know** – Students think of and state all the knowledge they have on a subject.

• **W: What I want to find out** – Each student thinks of and writes on a sheet of paper what they want to learn from the reading.

• **L: What I learned** – After reading the text, students write what they have learnt.

Building Vocabulary and Concepts

• To read effectively, readers need knowledge of word meanings and must have adequate vocabulary knowledge.

• Vocabulary knowledge and the ability to understand the concepts of words are related to reading achievement.

- Concepts are commonly explained as ideas, abstractions, or the essence of things.

Expanding Vocabulary

- Highlighting multiple word meanings: Multiple meaning words often cause confusion in reading.
- Example: **there** – one meaning indicates place; another begins statements (There are five oceans).
- **Spot** – a verb meaning "to locate" and a noun as in "spots on the dog."
- **Miss** – can convey different meanings: missing a bus, missing someone, a purse gone missing.
- To enhance understanding of multiple-meaning words, use sentence completion exercises highlighting differences in use.

Providing Concrete Experiences

- Specially effective for young learners who can be taught vocabulary through experience.
- Experiences could be doing actions to learn verbs, going on a nature walk to learn names of things in nature, reinforcing new vocabulary through pictures in books.
- As students progress, teachers can foster skills of classifying.

Cloze Procedure

• The cloze procedure is a useful technique for building comprehension and language skills.

• First select a passage of reading material.

• Rewrite the material and delete every fifth word, replacing it with a blank line.

• Students fill in the blanks with suitable words that match the context.

Sub-skills to Be Emphasized in Comprehension

Main Idea and Supporting Details

• Recognizing the main idea helps in understanding the central concept of the passage.

Recognizing Details

• Focus on looking at relevant details in the reading passage.

• Details help answer Wh- questions: Who, What, When, Where, Which, How, Why.

• Children should look for and highlight details while reading.

• After reading, details should be recorded using a graphic organizer.

• Students can then answer questions with graphic organizer support.

Sequencing

• Understanding sequence in a text is an important reading skill.

• Passages may describe a sequence of events, a process, or cause and effect.

• Students should record sequence using a graphic organizer.

• Highlight words that indicate sequence: first, next, then, finally, lastly.

Summarizing

• This stage is reached after the main idea, details and sequence are understood.

• Summarizing helps students focus on the important points of the passage.

• Students demonstrate comprehension through summarizing.

• A graphic organizer or cloze passage can support summary writing.

Compare and Contrast

• A higher level of comprehension.

• Students need to find similarities and differences between ideas in the text.

• It requires identifying similar information and segregating different information.

• A Venn diagram is useful for illustrating similarities and differences.

Predicting Outcome / Inferencing

• A higher-level comprehension skill.

• The child brings experience and prior knowledge to make predictions or infer situations.

• Requires reading "between the lines."

• Students must find cues in the paragraph to support their inference.

• Encourage thinking aloud and justifying answers.

Finally...

• The effectiveness of any reading exercise is visible when prior planning has taken place.

• Reading exercises should be divided into tasks (task analysis) so the child receives reinforcement of known skills while learning new skills needed for task completion.

- Keep the interest of the child in mind.
- Use multisensory approaches to maintain engagement.
- Use resources like pictures, internet, labels, cut-outs, highlighters, and graphic organizers to make the exercise enjoyable.

DYSCALCULIA REMEDIAL STRATEGIES

LANGUAGE

Problems

- If dyslexic, the student will face difficulty reading the given sum.
- Too much information in a sum will confuse the student.
- Mathematical terms such as *take away, sum, difference, product, minus, subtract, prime factors, denominator, supplementary* confuse dyslexics.

Additional Problems

- The spoken language system can confuse learning-disabled students.
- In the term *twenty-six*, *ty* actually stands for *ten*.
- The terms in the *teens* should logically be "onety" series (e.g., *onety six* for sixteen).
- Story sums are the most difficult because students must read, understand, decide the operations, and remember the sequence of steps.

Strategies

- Use flashcards for all mathematical vocabulary.

- While reading sums, encourage oral reading.
- Let the child explain what they understood; if incorrect, guide the child through the sum.
- Always use simple language and avoid unnecessary detail in the sum.

Strategies (Story Sums)

- Start with easier story sums and include pictures for early learners.
- Highlight terms such as *numerator, reciprocal, total, altogether, take away, difference, in all, total, more, add, less.*
- Encourage identification of key words and the required operation.
- In higher classes, provide simpler versions of the story or algebraic sums.
- Ensure questions are well spaced.

PERCEPTION

Problems – Visual-Spatial Processing

- Loses place on the worksheet
- Difficulty seeing differences between numbers, coins, or operation symbols
- Difficulty writing in a straight line

● Difficulty with direction: up-down, left-right, aligning numbers, reversals

● Difficulty using a number line

● Difficulty recognizing that a math sum is the same vertically and horizontally

● Difficulty with graph-related activities

Problems – Auditory Processing

● Difficulty "counting on" from within a sequence

● Difficulty doing oral drills

Strategies – Visual Processing

● Use squared paper.

● Ask the student to point to letters and numbers while reading (especially primary classes).

● Highlight important terms such as *difference, expand*.

● Use colour coding.

● Highlight symbols such as +, >, %, Σ.

● Use concrete objects in elementary classes.

● Use diagrams, flashcards, formula charts, graphs, and simpler examples.

ATTENTION

Problems

- Difficulty maintaining attention during sums
- Difficulty doing multi-step story sums
- Difficulty sustaining attention during instruction

Strategies

- Provide fewer sums per page.
- Avoid unnecessary details.
- Teach self-correction strategies.
- Help reduce *math anxiety*.
- Provide breaks during sessions.
- Use rough sheets.
- Provide short, repeated instructions.
- Offer steps in a flowchart format.

NUMBER PROCESSING

Problems

- Difficulty understanding the relationship between a number and its value (e.g., "2" represents two objects).
- Difficulty understanding number sequences.

- Difficulty understanding place value.

- Difficulty understanding number systems such as fractions, decimals, Roman numerals, rational numbers, integers, whole numbers.

Strategies – One-to-One Correspondence

Use identical objects initially; introduce different objects later.

Examples:

- Give one pencil to each child
- Match each head to a hat
- Match each coin to a marble

Strategies – Matching

Identical matching involves combining "similar" objects (e.g., pair of red socks).

Sorting helps develop classification skills.

Example: Ask the child to group 4 capsicums and 1 orange by sorting vegetables.

Strategies – Ordering

● Ask what comes after 8, before 15, or between 5 and 7.

● Introduce number lines to visualize sequence.

● In higher classes, introduce number patterns: e.g., 3, 6, 9... explain subtracting the starting number and then adding repeatedly.

Counting

Problems

● Children often learn counting by rote; pointing to objects may not be enough.

● Difficulty transitioning between 9→10, 19→20, etc.

● Use flashcards and constant revision.

● A number line supports these transitions.

Strategies

● Use motor activities such as writing numbers on steps and having the child jump on them.

● Use rhymes, poems, and songs.

● Practice transitions frequently.

Number Concepts

● Use concrete objects (e.g., Jodo cubes) to teach ascending/descending order.

● Teach counting digits in numbers; compare starting from the leftmost digit.

● Use number lines for equal spacing and understanding increases.

● Teach Number Bonds. Start with 10, extend to 100, 1000.

Example – Number Bonds of 10

9	8	7	6	5	4	3	2	1
1	2	3	4	5	6	7	8	9

Place Value Strategies

● Use Dienes blocks.

● Always write place values above digits.

● Include activities:

- Expanded form
- Number names
- Biggest/smallest number from digits
- Teach children to read numbers from right to left for place identification.

Addition Strategies

- Use concrete objects and pictures.
- Use number lines.
- Teach **a + 0 = a**.
- Teach the commutative rule: **a + b = b + a**.

Additional Strategies

- Adding on 9 (first add 10, then subtract 1).
- Use doubles: 8+8=16, 7+7=14.
- Near doubles: 8+7 = 15.
- Encourage number bonds for quick mental math.

Strategies – Adding to 10

- Teach that adding to 10 is simple-only the tens place increases.
- Teach vertical and horizontal addition.
- Write place values above numbers.
- Use lined or square paper.

Subtraction Strategies

- Discuss subtraction facts alongside addition facts.

Example:

5 + 3 = 8

8 - 3 = 5

- Teach borrowing and carrying using concrete objects.
- Use colours to differentiate large and small numbers in borrowing.

Example: Subtract 48 from 72.

MULTIPLICATION

Problems

- Difficulty learning tables
- Difficulty with direction
- Difficulty placing a zero in sums like 134 × 12

Strategies

- Explain multiplication as repeated addition.
- Teach easier methods: flashcards, doubling, skip counting on 2, 5, 10.

- Teach the commutative property: **2 × 3 = 3 × 2.**
- Teach direct products such as 21×100, 45×20, 56×1000.
- Colour the place of the cross or zero in early stages.

Division

- Tables
- Difficulty with direction of solving and placing numbers in the correct places
- Confusion with the terms divisor, quotient, dividend, remainder
- Difficulty dividing by 50, 200, 1500

Strategies

- Teach that division is repeated subtraction.
- Initially teach division with concrete objects. Ask the child to share or divide the number of pencils, counters, etc.
- After the manipulative phase, teach written division. For example: 520 ÷ 5. Many children may incorrectly write 14.
- Teach the formula for checking division.
- Use vertical squared paper in the initial stages since alignment of numbers is critical.

• Children with weak spatial ordering may find written division very difficult.

• Teach that division can be represented in more than one way.

Fractions

• Understanding the meaning: How can two quantities represent one value?

• New terms used in this concept

• Equivalent fractions

• Addition and subtraction of unlike fractions

• Division of fractions

• Converting improper fractions to mixed numbers and vice versa

Strategies

• Introduce the concept using pictures and real-life examples such as chocolate bars and pizza slices.

• Explain the concept of equivalent fractions using visual models.

• Explain numerator, denominator, reciprocal, half, quarter, etc.

• Highlight "L.C.M." when adding or subtracting unlike fractions initially.

• Number the steps of converting mixed fractions to improper and vice versa.

Time

• Words such as quarter, time after, and time before are confusing

• Conversion between 12-hour and 24-hour formats

• Addition and subtraction of hours, minutes, and seconds

• Conversion between hours–minutes and minutes–seconds

Strategies

• Teach time using a clock as a visual aid. Show all hands and their movement.

• First teach time in hours, then half past the hour.

• Teach quarter past and quarter to.

• Teach minutes past and minutes to.

• Let the child physically experience duration (e.g., 1 minute, 5 minutes).

• Teach units of hour, minute, and second clearly.

• Do conversion problems (hour to minutes, minutes to seconds, etc.).

• Teach both 12-hour and 24-hour clock systems.

• Provide addition and subtraction problems involving time. Go slowly-time calculation is difficult.

Decimals

• Understanding place value, including ones and tenths

• Conversion between fractions and decimals and vice versa

• Addition and subtraction of decimals

• Placement of decimal points in multiplication (10, 100, 1000, etc.)

• Division of decimals is especially difficult

Strategies

• Teach addition and subtraction of decimals and whole numbers, emphasizing decimal place alignment.

• Explain that decimal points in multiplication do not line up. Perform the multiplication normally, then count the total number of decimal places in the question to place the decimal correctly in the answer.

• Teach multiplication and division of decimals by 10, 100, 1000, etc., and how the decimal point moves to make the number larger or smaller.

Integers and Algebra

- Understanding positive and negative numbers
- Understanding the number line
- Applying the rules involving +, –, ×, ÷
- Understanding brackets
- Confusion with terms such as like and unlike terms, factorize, substitute, simplify, solve, expand, remove the bracket
- Understanding the difference between expressions such as:
- a × a × a
- a + a + a
- Understanding types and degrees of polynomials
- Adding, subtracting, multiplying, and dividing algebraic expressions

Strategies

- Explain integers using number lines.
- Teach rules of addition, subtraction, multiplication, and division using flashcards.
- Allow practice with only one type of sum initially.
- Emphasize understanding mathematical language in algebra.

• Teach technical terms clearly: like and unlike terms, factorize, substitute, simplify, expand, remove brackets. Highlight these initially and ask students to explain them before attempting sums.

• Teach the difference between multiplication of like terms (a × a × a) and repeated addition (a + a + a).

• Teach types and degrees of polynomials.

Strategies

• Teach addition and subtraction of algebraic expressions (combine only like terms, align vertically where needed).

• Teach both vertical and horizontal addition and subtraction.

• Teach solving linear equations using a balance method in the initial stage.

Procedural Skills

Problems

• Difficulty remembering steps involved in solving math problems

• Difficulty understanding patterns and sequences

• Difficulty organizing multi-step problems; needs tasks broken into sub-steps

Strategies

- Teach pattern sums involving sequences (counting by 2s, 3s, 5s, 10s).
- Before multi-step problems, ensure the child is confident with one-step problems.
- Break multi-step problems into small steps using flow charts and diagrams.
- Emphasize completing one step at a time and grade each step separately.
- Use mnemonics to remember steps.

Mathematical Reasoning

Strategies

- As this is a very difficult area for LD students, teach the following steps:

UNDERSTAND the problem – Extract important information and identify what is missing.

PLAN the solution – Use different approaches, diagrams, tables, and logical reasoning.

SOLVE the problem – Break the problem into smaller parts; solve unknown quantities using algebra, graphs, sound reasoning, etc.

CHECK the solution – Verify the answer, interpret results, and generalize strategies to new situations.

Strategies

- Always start with easier problems and explain how the solution is reached.
- Gradually increase difficulty while ensuring success; avoid giving difficult sums too early.
- Constantly motivate the child through the process.
- Ask reflective questions:
- Why do you think that?
- Can you explain why that is right?
- How do you know?
- How did you reach that conclusion?
- What might explain that?
- Provide lots of practice.

General Tips

- Identify the child's current level of functioning.
- Reduce math anxiety; encourage positive self-talk.
- Encourage deriving the correct answer on the first attempt.
- Teach self-correction.
- Praise the work (not the learner).
- Work in smaller groups or individually when possible.

- Allow more time to solve.
- Use calculators when appropriate.
- Give short, simple, repeated instructions.
- Provide ample practice and revision.
- Be patient.

General Tips

- Focus on one concept at a time.
- Keep language simple.
- Ensure practice questions are well spaced.
- Revisit topics regularly to build memory and confidence.
- Help the child develop independence-avoid constant spoon-feeding.

INDIVIDUALISED EDUCATION PROGRAM (IEP)

An Individualized Education Plan (or Program) is also known as an IEP. This is a plan or program developed to ensure that a child with an identified disability who is attending an elementary or secondary educational institution receives specialized instruction and related services.

The IEP creates an opportunity for teachers, parents, school administrators, related services personnel, and students (when appropriate) to work together to improve educational results for children with disabilities. The IEP is the cornerstone of a quality education for each child with a disability.

An IEP typically includes the following:

• The involvement and progress of the child with a disability in the general curriculum.

• All related services for which the child qualifies.

• Appropriate educational accommodations necessary for the child to be successful.

• The child's present levels of educational performance.

• Measurable annual goals and objectives for the child's education.

EIGHT Basic Components of an Individualized Education Program

Current Skill Level of the Student

Every IEP must include a description of your child's current performance and skills in all areas of concern. It should explain how the disability affects their progress in the general education curriculum. It will also assess their *functional performance* in non-academic areas like motor skills, behavior, and interpersonal relationships.

IEP teams typically use formal assessments to determine how your child is doing and establish a baseline of performance. The team may also use anecdotal information and feedback from teachers to further describe their skills.

Annual Goals

The IEP must contain information about your child's goals, which need to be updated at least once a year. Depending on what challenges your child faces, goals can relate to academic performance, behavior, improving their physical mobility in navigating between classes, and more.

Each objective should be measurable. With the help of regular evaluations, teachers and parents should be able to see how close a child has come to reaching their goals by the end of a school year.

Progress Tracking

The IEP must explain exactly how progress toward your child's goals will be measured, whether it is through regular testing or feedback reports from teachers. This gives you a clear idea of how your child is being evaluated throughout the year and provides reassurance that you will be kept informed about your child's achievements and setbacks.

Special Education Services

The IEP must clearly describe the student's special education program and how it has been designed to suit their particular needs. This includes details like separate instruction time, the use of one-on-one aides, and even special faculty training to help teachers learn more about how to best support your child.

Duration of Services

The IEP must include a projected beginning and end date of any services the IEP team proposes. This includes details on the frequency of the services and where they will be delivered. The intent is to ensure that everyone understands exactly when and where the student's individual program will take place.

Participation in Mainstream Classrooms

This section ensures that supportive staff and faculty are doing all they can to keep your child in the *least restrictive environment* as possible. With an aim of inclusion, this part of the IEP will detail how the child can join the general, mainstream classroom environment whenever it's appropriate.

The IEP must specify the amount of time a student will participate in these mainstream classes. It will also explain the rationale for that decision.

An IEP is a team effort: Several people need to collaborate to write it and then implement it. They include teachers, the specialist who evaluated your child as needing support services, a representative of the school system (usually a special education coordinator or a principal), and you and your co-parent.

Testing Adaptations

The IEP must explain if a child will participate in state and local achievement tests that other kids at their school take. If they will, it is important that the IEP specifies what types of *testing accommodations* will be used for the student. Testing accommodations might include extra time, distraction-free rooms, and wheelchair-accessible tests.

If you and teachers decide it is best that your child take modified or different tests to assess achievement, the rationale for that decision must be included in the IEP.

Transitional Goals and Services

An IEP is designed to help your child succeed in the present, but also prepare them for the next phase of their education. For that reason, starting around a child's 14th birthday, an IEP must include plans for transitioning a child beyond grade school.

Transitional goals and services focus on instruction and support services needed to help your child move from the school environment and into a job, vocational program, or another program designed to promote independent living. If your child aspires to go to college, the IEP should also include steps to help prepare them for advocating themselves in that environment.

NOTE

For a child who learns differently or has a disability, navigating just a single school day-much less an entire year-can be overwhelming. But a well-designed IEP can identify manageable goals that can reassure and motivate a child.

An IEP is an integral part of the special education process and should be written with care. If an IEP is required for your child, be sure you understand what it should include (and why). Ask questions of the IEP team and hold educators accountable for closely monitoring your child's progress and keeping you updated. In many ways, you captain the IEP process, and your attention to detail can be key to the plan's-and your child's-success.

Who Needs an IEP?

Students struggling in school may qualify for support services, allowing them to be taught in a special way, for reasons such as:

- learning disabilities
- **attention deficit hyperactivity disorder (ADHD)**
- emotional disorders
- cognitive challenges
- **autism**
- **hearing impairment**
- **visual impairment**
- **speech or language impairment**
- developmental delay
- physical disabilities

Signs that a student may have a learning disability include:

- getting poor grades despite significant effort
- needing continual, step-by-step guidance for tasks
- not being able to remember problem-solving steps because the child does not understand the tasks or the logic behind them
- having poor memory of spoken or written material

• having difficulty mastering tasks or transferring academic skills to other tasks

• not being able to remember skills and facts over time

• having strong general knowledge, but not being able to read (**dyslexia**), write (**dysgraphia**), or do math (**dyscalculia**) at that level

• having difficulty with **communication and language processing**, expressive language, or receptive language

• being extremely frustrated with school and homework

How Are Services Delivered?

• In most cases, services outlined in an IEP can be provided in regular education classrooms.

• In other cases, IEP services may be delivered in separate resource classrooms or separate schools, depending on the student's needs.

• Some students may have an IEP for one subject area only; others may have one for all academic subjects plus social skills instruction.

The **least restrictive setting** for students with IEPs is a regular education classroom. Students usually join regular classes for subjects such as science, social studies, art, music, library, gym, and health. It is critical that regular classroom teachers read and understand the IEP and monitor the services required in the plan.

The next least restrictive setting is a **resource or learning support classroom**, where small-group instruction is given by a certified special education teacher. Additional aides may assist with teaching.

Students who need intense intervention may be taught in **special schools** with fewer students per teacher and more individualized attention.

Evaluation and Referral

The referral process begins when a teacher, parent, or doctor is concerned that a child may be having trouble in the classroom.

The first step is to gather specific data regarding the student's progress or academic problems. This may include:

- a conference with parents
- a conference with the student
- observations of the student
- analysis of performance (attention, behavior, work completion, tests, classwork, homework)

This information helps school personnel determine the next step. Strategies specific to the student may be used to help the child become more successful before any formal testing. If the student continues to struggle, testing for a specific learning disability or other impairment may be recommended.

A disability alone does not guarantee services. To be eligible, the disability must **affect functioning at school**.

To determine eligibility, a **multidisciplinary team** evaluates the child based on observations, standardized tests, classwork, quizzes, and homework.

Who's On the Team?

The evaluation team can include:

- classroom teachers
- a psychologist
- a physical therapist
- an occupational therapist
- a speech therapist
- a special educator
- a vision or hearing specialist
- others, depending on the child's needs

After determining that further testing is required, parents will sign a permission form outlining who is involved and what tests will be used. Tests may assess reading, math, speech, language, or general developmental skills. Testing does not automatically mean a child will receive services.

Once assessments are completed, the team prepares a **Comprehensive Evaluation Report (CER)** summarizing findings and educational classification, and outlining needed skills and support.

Parents review the report before the IEP is developed. If they disagree, they can work with the school to create a plan that best meets the child's needs.

Who's On the Team?

• The professionals on the evaluation team can include:

• classroom teachers

• a psychologist

• a physical therapist

• an occupational therapist

• a speech therapist

• a special educator

• a vision or hearing specialist

• others, depending on the child's specific needs

- After it is determined that further testing is necessary, parents will be asked to sign a permission form that will detail who is involved in the process and the types of tests they use. These tests might include measures of specific school skills, such as reading or math, as well as more general developmental skills, such as speech and language. Testing does not necessarily mean that a child will receive services.
- Once the team members complete their individual assessments, they develop a

comprehensive evaluation report (CER) that compiles their findings, offers an educational classification, and outlines the skills and support the child will need.

- The parents then have a chance to review the report before the IEP is developed. If parents disagree with the report, they will have the opportunity to work together with the school to come up with a plan that best meets the child's needs.

Developing an IEP

• The next step is an IEP meeting, during which the team and parents decide what will go into the plan. Also, a regular classroom teacher should attend to offer suggestions about how the plan can help the child's progress in the standard education curriculum and how it can be used in a regular classroom setting, if that's appropriate.

- At the meeting, the team will discuss a student's educational needs - as described in the CER - and come up with specific, measurable short-term and annual goals for each of those needs.
- The cover page of the IEP outlines the related services and supports students will receive and how often they will be provided. These can include many different things; for example, transportation; speech-language pathology and audiology services; psychological services; physical and occupational therapy; recreation,

including therapeutic recreation; social work services; and medical services (for diagnostic and evaluation purposes only).

- If the team recommends several services, the amount of time they take in the child's school schedule can seem overwhelming. To ease that load, some services may be provided on a consultative basis. In these cases, the professional consults with the teacher to come up with strategies to help the child but doesn't offer any hands-on instruction. For instance, an occupational therapist may suggest accommodations for a child with fine-motor problems that affect handwriting, and the classroom teacher would incorporate these suggestions into the handwriting lessons taught to the entire class.
- Other services can be delivered right in the classroom, so the child's day isn't interrupted by therapy. The child who has difficulty with handwriting might work one-on-one with an occupational therapist while everyone else practices their handwriting skills. When deciding how and where services are offered, the child's comfort and dignity should be a top priority.
- If a child has academic needs and is working below grade level, services may be offered outside the regular education classroom, with students getting small-group instruction in a particular subject area (usually language arts or

math) by a special education teacher with other students who have similar needs.

- The IEP should be reviewed annually to update the goals and ensure the levels of service meet the student's needs. During the school year, progress monitoring will be done often to make sure the student is achieving goals set in the IEP. IEPs can be changed at any time on an as-needed basis.
- Specific timelines ensure that the development of an IEP moves from referral to providing services as quickly as possible. Be sure to ask about this timeframe and stay informed.
- If parents disagree with any part of the CER or the IEP, mediation and hearings are options.
- It is important for teachers to understand the IEP process and their role in delivering instruction to students who have an IEP. Any questions related to an IEP can be directed to the SEN team or the special education teacher assigned to a student.

IEP Planning Form – Sample

IEP Objectives	Arrival	Journal Writing	Recess	Language Arts	Lunch	Physical Education	Social Studies	Science	Dismissal
Develop Social Skills	Practice greeting people by name	Use communication book with teacher assistant	Participate in organized games	Take part in co-op reading group	Practice courtesy rules during eating and socializing	Practice taking turns	Work at center with peer helper	Work at center with peer helper	Line up with friends to wait for parent
Improve Decision Making	Choose place in line	Pick topic from communication book	Pick between two games	Choose book for group to read	Decide order to eat food	N/A	Decide between two centers	Decide between two centers	Choose who to stand with in line
Staying on Task	Complete routine of storing belongings	Stay on task for 10 minutes	Stay with the game chosen	Remain in groups and finish activity	Finish lunch and remain seated for 15 minutes	Stay in group for activity	Stay in each center for at least 10 minutes	Stay in each center for at least 10 minutes	Complete routines of retrieving all belongings and bring work home
Participating in Group Activities	Enter with classmates	N/A	Play with classmates	Answer questions about story	Help with clean-up in groups	Play with peers	Peer pairs	Peer pairs	Exit with classmates
Lengthen Interacting Behavior	Extend interaction with peer from communication book	Connect interaction from the communication book	Stay with peers and join in	Use more interaction in book to answer questions	N/A	Practice gesture communication with peers in group	Increase peer sessions to 15 minutes	Increase peer sessions to 15 minutes	N/A

Nine Types of Adaptions

Input	Output	Time
Adapt the way instruction is delivered to the learner. *For example:* Use different visual aids; plan more concrete examples; provide hands-on activities; place students in cooperative groups.	Adapt how the learner can respond to instruction *For example:* Allow a verbal vs. written response; use a communication book for students; allow students to show knowledge with hands-on materials.	Adapt the time allotted and allowed for learning, task completion or testing. *For example:* Individualize a timeline for completing a task; pace learning differently (increase or decrease) for some learners.

Difficulty	Level of Support	Size
Adapt the skill level, problem type, or the rules on how the learner may approach the work. *For example:* Allow a calculator for math problems; simplify task directions; change rules to accommodate learner needs.	Increase the amount of personal assistance with specific learner. *For example:* Assign peer buddies, teaching assistants, peer tutors or cross-age tutors.	Adapt the number of items that the learner is expected to learn or compete. *For example:* Reduce the number of social studies terms a learner must learn at any one time.

Degree of Participation	Alternate Goals	Substitute Curriculum
Adapt the extent to which a learner is actively involved in the task. *For example:* In geography, have a student hold the globe, while others point out the locations.	Adapt the goals or outcome expectations while using the same materials. *For example:* In social studies, expect one student to be able to locate just the states while others learn to locate capitals as well.	Provide the different instruction and materials to meet a learner's individual goals. *For example:* Individualize a timeline for completing a task; pace learning differently (increase or decrease) for some learners.

CONCLUSION

Lighting Pathways for Every Learner

As we arrive at the end of *Sitaare Zameen Par*, we return to the central truth that shaped every chapter: each child is a universe of potential, waiting to be understood, nurtured, and guided toward growth. Across these pages, we explored the layered complexity of learning-from the earliest foundations of oral language to the sophisticated cognitive processes behind writing, reading, spelling, mathematics, and individualized instruction. What becomes clear is that no child struggles in isolation; their challenges are woven through systems of language, perception, cognition, attention, environment, and emotional wellbeing. Understanding this interconnectedness is what allows us to transform learning from a series of tasks into a journey of empowerment.

Throughout this book, we have traveled through the intricate architecture of human learning: the delicate movements required for handwriting, the sequencing and memory involved in reading, the patterns and logic that structure mathematics, and the expressive and receptive skills that give language meaning. These domains are not independent silos. They behave like constellations-separate points that form clearer pictures only when viewed together. When a child hesitates before writing, misreads a passage, loses their place in a subtraction exercise, or misunderstands a word problem, it is rarely a sign of low ability. Far more often, it is a signal that one of the underlying systems needs support, clarity, or re-teaching in a way that aligns with their learning profile.

The heart of this book has always been to help adults-teachers, parents, specialists, and caregivers-see these signals for what they are: calls for compassion, adaptation, and thoughtful intervention. It takes courage to step away from rigid academic expectations and choose instead to observe, listen, and adjust. Yet this courage is what creates inclusive, thriving classrooms. When we give children the space to show what they know in different ways, when we scaffold instead of criticize, when we replace fear with curiosity, we do more than improve academic performance-we reshape their belief in themselves.

From Understanding to Action

The strategies presented in this book are not merely instructional suggestions; they are pathways toward equitable learning. Whether you are implementing phonics instruction, teaching morphological awareness, building spelling through rules and patterns, supporting slow processors through graphic organizers, or breaking down math concepts into manageable steps, each action becomes a lifeline for a child. The most effective learning environments are those where the adults are willing to examine *how* a child learns rather than focusing only on *what* they learn.

Children thrive when they are taught through meaningful experiences-writing that begins with ideas they care about, reading that connects to their own lives, math that links to real-world logic, and language tasks that reflect authentic communication. They grow when instruction honors their pace, celebrates their strengths, and scaffolds their challenges. They become confident when learning feels achievable, not overwhelming.

The Role of Empathy and Observation

Every chapter of this book has emphasized the role of the adult as an observer-a person who pays attention to the subtleties of behavior, effort, and response. The teacher who notices a child gripping a pencil too tightly or losing track during multi-step directions holds the key to meaningful intervention. The parent who senses frustration building during homework can shift the environment, break down tasks, or seek support. The counselor who identifies gaps in expressive language can collaborate with the teacher to adjust expectations.

Empathy is not a soft skill in education; it is the foundation on which all effective teaching rests. A child who feels understood learns more willingly. A child who feels safe attempts tasks they once avoided. And a child who trusts the adults around them becomes an active participant in their own growth. In this sense, empathy is not just emotional support-it is a pedagogical strategy.

Collaboration: The Strength of the System

No single adult-teacher, parent, therapist-can meet every need on their own. That is why collaborative systems like IEPs, multidisciplinary evaluations, and regular communication between school and home are vital. When professionals share insights, when parents articulate observations, and when schools create structures for consistent monitoring, the child benefits from a cohesive, informed support network.

This book has underlined the importance of teamwork-speech therapists who guide language development, occupational therapists who strengthen graphomotor skills, special educators who design targeted goals, general educators who adapt classroom practices, and families who reinforce learning at home. Each person brings a unique lens, and together, they create a comprehensive understanding of the child's learning journey.

Celebrating Progress, Not Perfection

It is essential to remember that learning is rarely linear. Children grow in uneven patterns-rapid improvement followed by plateaus, breakthroughs mixed with setbacks. This is not failure; it is the natural rhythm of development. The true measure of progress lies in confidence gained, habits strengthened, strategies internalized, and resilience built through every challenge.

When a child who once avoided writing begins jotting ideas independently...

When a hesitant reader starts volunteering to read aloud...

When a child who struggled with number sense begins solving problems using visual strategies...

When a child becomes aware of their own learning needs and asks for help appropriately...

These are victories worth celebrating. These are the moments that shape lifelong learners.

A New Way of Seeing Children

Perhaps the greatest shift this book hopes to inspire is a new way of seeing children-not as empty vessels to be filled with knowledge, but as dynamic, capable individuals navigating a world that often demands more than their developing systems can handle. When we slow down, observe, and personalize instruction, we allow each child's identity, curiosity, and intelligence to guide the learning process.

The stars in the night sky do not shine with equal intensity, nor do they follow the same patterns. Yet each contributes to the beauty and meaning of the constellation. In the same way, every child brings a unique brightness to the classroom-one that may not always align with conventional expectations, but one that is deeply worthy of recognition.

A Final Reflection

As you close this book, may you carry forward not just strategies, but a mindset-one that values patience over pressure, understanding over assumption, and growth over perfection. May you look at every child-whether struggling or soaring-and ask not, "Why can't they do this?" but "What do they need to succeed?" And may you remember that your belief in a child can become the single most transformative force in their academic and emotional life.

In the end, *Sitaare Zameen Par* is both a guide and a reminder:

Children are not defined by their struggles.

They are defined by the potential that emerges when someone believes in them.

Our job, as the adults entrusted with their learning, is simply this - **to notice their light, nurture it with care, and help it shine across the sky.**

The End

9 789355 920256

Printed at Repro India Ltd.